BERLITZ®

BAHAMAS

11th edition (1992/1993)

Updated or revised 1992, 1991, 1988, 1987, 1984, 1982, 1981

How to use our guide

- All the practical information, hints and tips that you will need before and during the trip start on page 105.

- For general background, see the sections The Islands and the People, p. 6, and A Brief History, p. 12.

- All the sights to see are listed between pages 22 and 74, with a special section on Florida on pages 75 to 86. Our own choice of sights most highly recommended is pinpointed by the Berlitz traveller symbol.

- Entertainment, nightlife and all other leisure activities are described between pages 86 and 99, while information on restaurants and cuisine is to be found on pages 100 to 104.

- Finally, there is an index at the back of the book, pp. 126–128.

Found an error or an omission in this Berlitz Guide? Or a change or new feature we should know about? Our editor would be happy to hear from you, and a postcard would do. Be sure to include your name and address, since in appreciation for a useful suggestion, we'd like to send you a free travel guide. Write to: Berlitz Publishing Co. Ltd., London Road, Wheatley, Oxford OX9 1YR, England.

    Although we make every effort to ensure the accuracy of all the information in this book, changes occur incessantly. We cannot therefore take responsibility for facts, prices, addresses and circumstances in general that are constantly subject to alteration.

Text: Don Larrimore
Photography: Daniel Vittet (pp. 2–3, Chris McLaughlin)
Layout: Aude Aquoise
We're particularly grateful to William Kalis, Eric Wilmott, Joseph Edwards and Larry Smith, Bahamas News Bureau, for their help in the preparation of this book. We also wish to thank the Bahamas Tourist Office for their valuable assistance.
Cartography: ⦿ Falk-Verlag, Hamburg.

Contents

Cover picture: View over the beach on Harbour Island

The Islands and the People

Strewn over a vast expanse of the Atlantic ocean, the Bahamas bask in breezy, semi-tropical sunshine. Out of about 700 islands, over 100 are at least minimally inhabited though only some two dozen have vacation facilities. Apart from birds, turtles and an occasional iguana, the other 2,400 smaller cays (pronounced 'keys') of the Commonwealth of the Bahamas* are deserted.

The great glory of these islands is the incredible sea they ornament. Colors range from pale crystal green in the Great and Little Bahama Banks to regal blue in Exuma Sound and the awesomely deep Tongue of the Ocean. The water is so clear you hardly need a snorkel mask to enjoy the astonishing array of marine life at countless coral reefs. Divers can explore fish-filled blue holes and seek the wrecks of the many treasure ships which came to grief over centuries in the treacherous shoals of what the Spaniards called *baja mar* (shallow sea). From that came the anglicized name, Bahamas.

Starting as close as 50 miles to the Florida coast, the Bahamas archipelago swoops southeast for some 600 miles almost to Haiti and eastern Cuba. This strategic location, along the major shipping routes between the Caribbean and North America, has been a crucial factor in the history of the islands. Ever since Chris-

* The total land area of the Bahamas is about 5,380 square miles, making the territory slightly smaller than Hawaii, or about half the size of Belgium. The Commonwealth has 100,000 square miles of territorial waters.

topher Columbus came ashore on the Bahamian out island of San Salvador in 1492, wreckers, pirates, rum runners and modern smugglers have been among those who found the thousands of reefs, cays and coves useful.

The islands are flattened peaks of huge submarine mountains rising from the floor of the Atlantic ocean. They don't protrude very far above sea level—the highest point in the Bahamas, Mount Alvernia on Cat Island, is only 206 feet. Some of the surrounding banks are so shallow that at low tide they emerge from the water (to the delight of seashell buffs).

Once away from Nassau and Freeport, you'll have a hard time finding a crowd along the 630 miles of beaches fringing the Bahamian islands.

Size isn't a reliable guide to importance in the Bahamas. Andros, the largest island, is mostly wilderness, while more than half of the country's 210,000 citizens live on little New Providence Island, in or around Nassau, the capital. Some of the most charming islands have no more than a few hundred or a few thousand inhabitants. Here you'll find away-from-it-all resorts as attractive as any in the Mediterranean or the Caribbean. Life on these drowsy Family Islands (previously designated "Out Islands") is in great contrast to the near-metropolitan bustle of Nassau or the breezy brashness of the second major population center, Freeport on Grand Bahama Island.

Tourism is overwhelmingly the nation's biggest business, providing two-thirds of all local jobs. Nassau, Paradise Island, and Freeport have been designed for holiday pleasure, and are jam-packed much of the time with visitors determinedly pursuing it. That may mean anything from beach ambling to casino gambling, or snorkeling, golfing, sailing, tennis, scuba diving, bird watching, fishing, wind surfing, horseback riding, water skiing, para-sailing, squash or butterfly hunting. In some spots

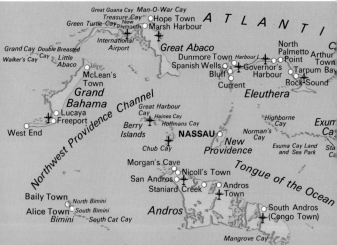

there's interesting shopping at surprising savings. Souvenir hunters will be delighted by the postage stamps and currency notes—among the prettiest in the world. Seafood dining can be rewarding, with or without the endless variety of rum drinks. After sundown, disco dancing and native entertainment get started.

For some Americans, the Bahamas, so close to Florida, gives the impression of a foreign country. It may be the architectural and ceremonial echoes of the British colonial era in downtown Nassau, the German and French signs in hotel lobbies or the everyday use of the word "roundabout" instead of traffic circle. Other travelers are more likely to be impressed by the Americanization of this island nation which gained political independence from Britain in 1973. "Who says Miami's not contagious?" is one quip about Freeport.

Sea, sun and sand are the perpetual lures for tourists. But the Bahamas has another major attraction. The nation is one of the world's leading tax havens, an offshore money center with some 350 licensed financial institutions. There are no income, capital gains, corporation, death or inheritance taxes and the bankers aren't

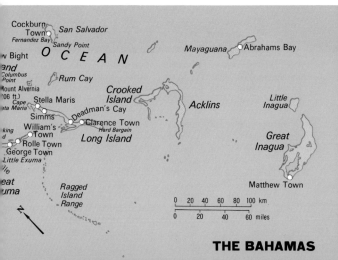

THE BAHAMAS

the only ones who appreciate the Swiss-style secrecy laws. "Tax havening" has now become the second largest industry.

Visitors most often find islanders affable and notably relaxed. "We have three speeds," you may hear a Bahamian explain, "slow, stop and reverse." While there's plenty of goodwill about being helpful to tourists, there is rarely any great hurry about getting **10** things done. Keeping an ap-

pointment on "Bahamian time" means arriving late by many minutes at least, if not hours or even days. Threatening or getting angry won't work, as Bahamians simply don't accept criticism as being fair.

But here, as on many another island in the sun, happiness is to shift down to low gear and drift with the languid local pace. To help you unwind, many settlements have an excellent informal institution

Inexpensive and plentiful: straw hats protect tourists and natives against the powerful Bahamas sun.

known as a "lazy" or "lazing" tree, usually an old silk cotton, almond or wild fig tree under which citizens spend a great deal of time sitting in the shade chatting quietly. Gossip is a favorite island pastime. Other enthusiasms are fairs and church picnics, dancing and singing to goombay and ca- lypso music (many Bahamians sing to themselves) and such sports as baseball and basket- ball.

This is a very young popula- tion: more than half of all Bahamians are under 20. The swarms of small children you'll see are enormously appealing, although the boom in births in a country suffering high unem- ployment has provoked grave concern about the future. While there's a certain casual- ness in attitude about formal **11** marital ties, Bahamians take religion seriously: the great majority attend church regularly, and it's said there are more churches per capita here than in any other nation. At various island hotels, you're liable to find that a well-meaning maid has left an open Bible in your room.

Just as the Bahamas are not in the Caribbean (despite frequent confusion abroad), so Bahamians consider themselves distinct from West Indians. Black Bahamians, who make up some 85 per cent of the native population, in fact have more ties with southern U.S. blacks than with Caribbean islanders. That remains true despite the thousands of legal and illegal immigrants who come here from poorer islands, notably Haiti. With such a mixture of peoples the language is great fun, a bewildering blend of modern American, colonial British, Caribbean creole, African slave and even pirate slang.

Nowadays on posters, brochures, television and T-shirts you find the slogan, "It's Better in the Bahamas." That's unquestionably true about the marine scene. But ask an islander why, and you may well get this reply: "Cuz we got no snow, no taxes and no ulcers."

A Brief History

Centuries before Columbus crossed the Atlantic looking for a westbound passage to the Orient, a peaceful people had settled in the Bahamas. Originally from South America, they had slowly island-hopped by dugout canoe up through the Caribbean surviving by cultivating modest crops and from what they caught from sea and shore. With simple tools the islanders carved attractive wooden pieces and crafted jewelry. Wearing only a minimum of clothing, they painted their bodies for protection against the sun, insects and evil spirits.

Nothing in the experience of these gentle Indians* could have prepared them for the arrival of the *Pinta*, the *Niña* and the *Santa Maria* at San Salva-

---

* Columbus mistakenly called them Indians believing that he had reached the East Indies. They later became popularly known as Lucayans, a Europeanization of their *Lukku-cairi* name for themselves, which meant "island people".

It's often forgotten that Columbus, honored at Nassau's Government House, never saw North America.

dor on October 12, 1492. The exact site of the first encounter between the islanders and the armor-bearing discoverers is in dispute but whichever beach it was, the explorer renamed the island San Salvador and claimed it for his royal Spanish patrons. But not finding the gold and other riches he was seeking, Columbus and his tiny fleet sailed out of the Bahamas toward neighboring Cuba after two weeks.

The Spaniards never bothered to settle in the Bahamas, but the number of shipwrecks attest that their galleons frequently passed through the archipelago en route to and from the Caribbean, Florida, Bermuda (which they discovered in 1503) and their home ports. As for the Lucayans, within 25 years all of them, perhaps some 30,000 people, were removed from the Bahamas to work—and die—in Spanish gold mines, farms and pearl fisheries on Hispaniola (Haiti), Cuba and elsewhere in the Caribbean.

English sea captains also came to know the beautiful but deserted Bahamian islands during the 17th century. England's first formal move was on October 30, 1629, when Charles I granted the Bahamas and a chunk of the American south

to his Attorney General, Sir Robert Heath. But nothing came of that, nor of a rival French move in 1633 when Cardinal Richelieu, the 17th-century French statesman, tried claiming the islands for France.

Colonization and Piracy

In 1648 a group of English Puritans from Bermuda led by William Sayle sailed to Bahamian waters and established the first permanent European settlement on an island they named Eleutheria, after the Greek word for freedom. The 70 colonists called themselves the Eleutherian Adventurers, but life was very difficult on Eleutheria (known today as Eleuthera) and the colony never flourished, though Sayle was long honored for the effort. In 1666 a smaller island (called Sayle's island) with a fine harbor was settled by Bermudans and renamed New Providence. It was later to become known as Nassau, capital of the Bahamas.

In 1670 six Lords Proprietors of Carolina were granted the Bahama islands by Charles II, but for nearly 50 years their weak governors on New Providence either couldn't or wouldn't suppress the piracy which raged through the archipelago. Then, in 1684, to avenge countless raids against their ships, the Spanish dispatched a powerful squadron from Cuba to attack Nassau. This sent the majority of the English settlers fleeing to Jamaica or Massachusetts, but didn't have much effect on the pirates.

Most feared of the 1,000 or more swashbucklers operating from the New Providence lair was Edward Teach, better known as Blackbeard. Today you can visit a tower east of Nassau named after him. Another two infamous pirates were women: Anne Bonney and Mary Read had exceptionally bloodthirsty reputations and are still remembered in the Bahamas. The pirates raided anything on the sea, living totally lawless—and often not very lengthy—lives. Moreover there was not always a clear distinction between pirates and privateers, the latter officially authorized by their governments to plunder enemy ships during time of war. But whatever they were called, anarchy and confusion were rampant throughout the whole area.

In 1718, shortly after the Bahamas became a crown colony, Captain Woodes Rogers, a renowned ex-privateer, was named the first royal governor. Arriving in Nassau with a powerful force and promising amnesty for surrender, he became a Bahamian legend by cleaning out many of the pirates and establishing some order. This incident inspired the national motto *Expulsis Piratis—Restituta Commercia* (Pirates Expelled—Commerce Restored), which was retained until 1971.

A few years later Rogers quit the islands only to return for a second time in 1729 after a period of bankruptcy and debtor's prison in England. Before he died in Nassau in 1732 he had summoned the Bahamas' first official Assembly, composed of 16 elected members for New Providence and four each for Harbour Island and Eleuthera. At this time, in all the Bahamas there were only about 2,000 settlers.

New Providence knew some spells of prosperity in the mid-18th century as privateering resumed with England at war with Spain. The town of Nassau was expanded and lasting improvements were made between 1760 and 1768 by another revered Governor, William Shirley from Massachusetts. One of the island's major thoroughfares still carries his name. **15**

The American Revolutionary War

When the 13 American colonies, enraged by the Stamp Tax, got into the war which eventually brought independence, the Bahamas somewhat reluctantly found itself on England's side. But reluctance dissolved as profits from privateering once again flowed into Nassau. This time the plundered vessels were American, but not all the victories were won by the privateers. On March 3, 1776, a rebel squadron under commodore Esek Hopkins arrived and occupied Nassau for two weeks, a bloodless undertaking which emptied the island's forts of arms and other military supplies. A smaller and equally nonviolent American operation against the town in January 1778 lasted less than three days.

As the colonies' war effort picked up steam, both France and Spain weighed in against the British. In May, 1782, New Providence surrendered to a large Spanish-American invasion fleet from Cuba and for the next year a Spanish governor ruled the Bahamas.

News traveled slowly in those days. The Treaty of Versailles in 1783 formally restored the Bahamas to the British, but

Peaceful and often in ruins today, forts recall bitter battles fought for control of the prized Bahamas.

actual liberation came through a famous escapade which would never have happened in the age of the telegraph. Lieutenant-Colonel Andrew Deveaux, a loyalist from South Carolina, sailed from Florida with six ships, picked up men and fishing boats at Harbour Island and Eleuthera, and "invaded" Nassau. Though vastly outnumbered and outgunned, Deveaux employed elaborate ruses with his little boats to give the impression to the Spanish defenders that his force was overpowering. The humiliating Spanish surrender is proudly recalled in Bahamian history, even though it was all unnecessary: the peace treaty had been signed the previous week.

Deveaux was the first of some 7,000 loyalists who, with slaves and the promise of land grants, came to the Bahamas from the southern American colonies in the wake of the English defeat in the Revolutionary War. This influx profoundly affected the islands. A number of prominent Bahamians today are descendants of

loyalists or their slaves. As a reward for his efforts, Deveaux was given acreage on both New Providence and Cat Island. Other loyalists set up cotton plantations on various islands, and slaves soon became the majority of the population.

Emancipation and Decline

In the 1780s well over 100 cotton plantations were founded and flourished around the Bahamas. Prosperity from the land finally seemed a possibility. But by the end of the century cotton had fallen victim to a devastating plague of chenille bugs and exhaustion of the weak soil. Most of the planters left the islands and depression returned, only partly relieved by wrecking, the habitual freelance business of salvaging cargo from the ships forever running aground in the dangerous Bahamian waters. (Some wrecked ships were deliberately misguided by lights on shore. Nassau harbor didn't have a proper lighthouse until 1816).

Nassau became a free port in 1787, sparking a certain surge in trading activity. Loyalists built a number of the attractive colonial-style homes and public buildings still standing today, and during the War of 1812, privateers enjoyed another profitable spell against American vessels.

Slavery in the Bahamas was not as widespread or as vicious as on many sugar islands in the Caribbean. Some slaves were voluntarily freed or sold their liberty by loyalist owners. After 1804, no slaves were imported into the Bahamas. By 1822, the first-ever registration counted 10,808 slaves on the 17 inhabited islands or island clusters. After Parliament in London abolished slavery in 1833, there was a transitional apprenticeship period of 5 years before all slaves in the colony became fully free on August 1, 1838. This included a few thousand slaves from ships captured by the Royal Navy. They were housed in specially founded settlements on New Providence and the Out Islands. You'll find traces of those modest communities today at Adelaide and Carmichael on New Providence.

Civil War Blockade Running

Over the centuries, trouble on the nearby American continent has often meant good news for the Bahamas. When Lincoln ordered a blockade of the southern states in 1861 after the outbreak of the Civil War, the Bahamas quickly boomed.

Nassau harbor was busy with ships unloading Confederate cotton and tobacco and taking aboard arms, medicine and manufactured goods, mainly from Europe, to be run back through the northern blockade. As the war went on, speedy and camouflaged contraband vessels were built to slip past the ever-increasing Federal patrols. Profits from blockade running were incredible, and Nassau went wild. But the extravagant parties and carefree spending stopped abruptly with the North's victory in 1865. Late the following year an immense hurricane sent a tidal wave over Hog Island (today Paradise Island), smashing Nassau's flimsy buildings and ruining crops. Other islands were also devastated. As the Bahamas sank back into economic doldrums, citizens turned to less romantic and barely rewarding agriculture, fishing or salt raking. The spread of lighthouses and decent navigational charts had crippled the old standby, the wrecking trade.

For a time a new fibre called sisal seemed promising. But Bahamian soil was too poor and Mexico grew a better plant. Neville Chamberlain, future British prime minister, took over his family's sisal operation on Andros in the 1890s. It failed, the natives said, because of that island's evil elves called chickcharnies. Hopes were raised, and also fizzled, over Bahamian citrus and pineapple. Sponging, another vitally important industry for thousands of islanders at the end of the 19th century, also had setbacks. A hurricane in 1839 drowned some 300 sponge fishermen in the "mud" off Andros, and a devastating fungoid some 40 years later killed almost all the sponges.

The 20th Century

Desperate for work, perhaps 20 per cent of the Bahamian population left to take construction jobs in Florida between the turn of the century and World War I. During that war hundreds of Bahamians saw active service with British forces. The islands suffered food shortages and a serious bank failure, but nothing more militarily threatening than rumors of German submarines operating offshore.

Prohibition brought gloom to millions of Americans, but for the Bahamas it brought the biggest bonanza in history. At the end of 1919, Congress passed the Volstead Act making it illegal to manufacture, sell or transport intoxicating beverages. The Bahamian islands (where the temperance crusade never had much of a chance) were perfectly placed to help thirsty Americans. And they did. For 14 years, until the controversial law was finally repealed, bootlegging changed Nassau, West End on Grand Bahama and Bimini beyond recognition. With just as much gusto as they'd shown in the past for wrecking, privateering and blockade running, Bahamians took to the seas with illegal liquor. Trying to outwit the U.S. Coast Guard was risky but enormously profitable. Fortunes were made by respected Bahamian families turned liquor merchants, rum-running boat captains, notorious American criminals, shady ladies and the Bahamas government (which collected duty on temporarily imported drink).

Liquor money bought Nassau better houses, churches, street lighting, water, roads, sewers, docks and hotels. The city's first gambling casino opened in 1920; the first daily air service from Miami (Pan American Airways) began in 1929; the yacht set decided Nassau was fashionable, and many wealthy Americans as well as Prohibition millionaires **19** bought land and built homes on the islands.

The three bad hurricanes of 1926, 1928 and 1929 only temporarily stopped the carnival during that heady period for Nassau. When it did end it came with a severe slump, triggered first by the worldwide depression and then by the repeal of Prohibition in 1933. Unemployment stalked again, despite the beginnings of the first significant tourism the Bahamas had known.

In some respects, World War II put the Bahamas on the international map. The colony was chosen to have two of the sites Britain leased to the United States under Franklin D. Roosevelt's "destroyers for bases" deal in 1940. Allied forces operated submarine-hunting and air-sea rescue stations on the islands; Royal Air Force pilots and Royal Navy frogmen were trained here, and much trans-Atlantic air traffic passed through the Bahamas.

Then, to the astonishment of the local populace, the Duke of Windsor, having given up his throne for an American divorcee ("the woman I love"), was named governor of the little colony in 1940. He and the Duchess remained until 1945. This may partly explain why numerous wealthy Europeans,

Today Nassau harbor is one of the world's leading cruise-ship stops.

displaced by the war, took up residence in the Bahamas.

In 1943 the Duke intervened in the investigation of the murder of Canadian multi-millionaire Sir Harry Oakes, a long-time benefactor of the Bahamas who gave his name to Nassau's first airfield. The sensational case, never solved, made world headlines for the Bahamas and is still discussed today.

After the construction of the first wartime American air bases on New Providence was completed, thousands of Bahamians left to work on farms and in factories in the United States, a migration that continued well into the postwar era. But employment opportunities finally began to grow at home.

From 1950 on, a promotion and development campaign under Sir Stafford Sands was hugely successful in attracting tourists to the Bahamas. Denied the sun, sand and sin of Cuba by Fidel Castro's takeover in 1959, hundreds of thousands of American vacationers chose the Bahamas. The influx was spurred by casino gambling, airport and har-

bor improvement on the major islands, the creation of the modern city of Freeport, resort hotel building and, last but most importantly, the advent of air-conditioning.

Under a new constitution in 1964, the colony was given internal self-government with a ministerial-parliamentary system. In 1967 elections, the Progressive Liberal Party was victorious, its leader Lyndon O, Pindling becoming premier. Following a constitutional conference in London, the Bahamas became fully independent on July 10, 1973, and is now a member of the United Nations and the Commonwealth.

What to See

New Providence

Yachts glide gingerly into cluttered marinas; barefoot children cruise resort beaches hawking shell necklaces to rows of oiled sunbathers; cruise-ship bargain hunters swarm through the straw market and Bay Street boutiques; camera-clicking holidaymakers bob and sway in overworked glass-bottom boats; honeymooners hold hands (and their breath) as the casino roulette wheels spin on and on.

Much the greatest concentration of high-powered vacation action in the Bahamas is here, not only in Nassau town but farther along the northern shore of New Providence Island at Cable Beach, and across the narrow Nassau harbor channel on Paradise Island. The national government and a sizeable slice of the international financial pie are here too, but above all, it's on New Providence that you'll find the Commonwealth's fun capital...

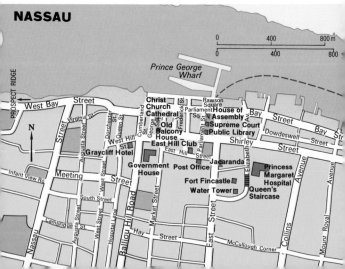

NASSAU

Nassau

With its hotel glitter and restaurant sophistication, its daytime traffic jams and nighttime naughtiness, Nassau is certainly not typical of the Bahamas. But it is a magnet.

Bay Street is the commercial center of the capital, crammed with shops, offices and crowds, but the traditional downtown tourist hub is the **straw market** on Market Plaza, at the corner with Frederick Street. There are massive displays of straw items, a type of inexpensive souvenir few visitors resist.

The amiably shrewd salesladies have been creating straw items since childhood. "You can make anyting outta straw if you just put your head to it," you'll hear. As you browse, you'll believe it. Best sellers are hats, dolls, bags and baskets. But watch for unusual straw airplanes and model surreys which are sometimes hard to find. Some of the best of the Bahamas' 200 woodcarvers also exhibit their craft here.

Conveniently facing Rawson Square's horse surrey station is the Central Tourist Information bureau, a friendly, comfortable and brochure-stocked refuge from the Bay Street bustle. Just beyond in Parliament Square, incongruous beneath the palm trees, stands a stout

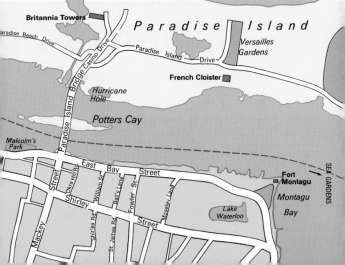

Shopping or strolling, you'll find most action here: Nassau's Bay St., busiest boulevard in the Bahamas.

red cylinder familiar to any Londoner. "That's the mail box," says the surrey driver to his customers as they clip-clop past. (Cautious local citizens prefer to use a post office.)

The picture-postcard **Public Buildings** dating from 1812 and a bleached marble statue of a young, seated Queen Victoria

in this area recall the British colonial era. Loyalist architects modeled Nassau's governmental complex after New Bern, capital of the North Carolina colony of two centuries ago. The present-day House of Assembly, parliamentary heart of the Bahamas, occupies the so-called western building. Nearby you'll see the Senate where Queen Elizabeth II made Bahamian history in 1977 by delivering her Silver Jubilee throne speech. Behind it at the

maps and portraits, a carved stone Arawak ceremonial stool and other artifacts. There are also some dramatic photographs of the damage done to Nassau in the 1929 hurricane.

Taking a brief stroll you'll find at least half a dozen other venerable buildings to admire, mostly from the outside. Up Parliament Street opposite the new Post Office is **Jacaranda,** a 140-year-old private residence partly built of ballast stones brought in from Georgia. Along East Hill Street stands the stately **East Hill Club,** built in the 1860s, which was once owned by Lord Beaverbrook.

A white statue of a dashing Columbus, in cape with walking stick, commands steep steps up to pink **Government House** (closed to the public), residence of governors and governor-generals for nearly two centuries. It occupies the top of a slight hill grandly called Mount Fitzwilliam. Every other Saturday morning there's a Changing of the Guard ceremony.

Privately owned **Balcony House** on Market Street, a photographer's favorite, was built by shipwrights in about 1790 of American soft cedar. It has a slave kitchen and a staircase thought to have been removed from a large vessel. **Christ Church Cathedral** (An-

newer Supreme Court the wigs and robes will remind you of the trappings of independence.

The oldest and most interesting building in this area is the **Public Library** between Shirley Street and the Court House. Built of stone in 1797, this octagonal edifice was a jail until 1873 when books replaced prisoners in the cells. The seashell collection in the entry has some rarities, but the really interesting things are upstairs where you can inspect fine old prints,

glican), on George Street, is a pleasantly airy building with a dark timbered roof setting off white pillars, modern stained glass, and wall tablets commemorating deaths from such past local scourges as yellow fever. Since 1670 there have been five churches on this site, two destroyed by Spanish raiders. The present building dates back to 1841, its prominent white tower even earlier. The three-storey **Deanery** on Cumberland Street, owned by the Anglican church, was erected about 1710 and may be the oldest complete residence in the Bahamas. Another well-preserved house is the impressive **Graycliff mansion** on West Hill Street where Winston Churchill's stay, some 60 years ago, is still recalled.

Returning to Shirley Street, walk east and then south up Elizabeth Avenue, until you come to the celebrated **Queen's Staircase,** an unusual sight. Slaves hacked the 65 steepish steps from the black rock cliff as a passageway for troops garrisoned above at Fort Fincastle. Ascending, you'll reach Nassau's water tower which of-fers the best **panorama** of New Providence, the harbor and Paradise Island. For a small entry fee you may take either the elevator or the stairs to the top of this white concrete tower. It's 216 feet above sea level, and the revolving green-white light is visible for 20 miles. The handful of modern skyscrapers you see sprouting from the flat, palm-studded landscape seem almost unreal. **Fort Fincastle,** which commands the promontory here above Princess Margaret Hospital, was built in 1793. There are five black cannons, but this mini-bastion has known few heroics.

Paradise Island

"Welcome to Paradise" says the sign just after you've paid your bridge toll. Pearly gates there aren't yet, but you immediately see tall casuarina trees and palms, which cover much of this renowned resort island. (*Note:* It's about eight times more expensive to take a vehicle over the bridge than to walk it in about 5 minutes. Otherwise, ferries ply quite often between the island and Rawson Square, but only during daylight hours.)

For centuries the 4 by half mile sliver of an islet was uninhabited, useful mainly as a

Imaginative yarns about the steps may be spun for gullible visitors.

weather shield for Nassau harbor. Known as Hog Island, it was bought before World War II by Swedish millionaire Axel Wenner-Gren for a private retreat. He sold out to American millionaire Huntington Hartford who decided the name Paradise was more likely than Hog to attract visitors to

his new seaside hotel. In recent years the island has been developed (primarily by a U.S. gambling-hotel organization) into a complete "destination within a destination," with hotels, a casino and cabaret, extensive sports facilities, a marina called Hurricane Hole where yacht-watching can be eyebrow-raising, and a seaplane airline. **Paradise Beach** is the best known of the excellent beaches strung out along the island's north shore.

Among the celebrities who've been here, multimillionaire recluse Howard Hughes was frequently in the headlines during his prolonged residence in a de luxe hotel. Years later, the Shah of Iran arrived shortly after being exiled and deposed.

The biggest bargain on Paradise is watching **dolphins** being fed in the mid-island lagoon near the Britannia Towers. This free half-hour show goes on twice daily, about 10 a.m. and 4 p.m. Two dolphins leap as high as 20 feet in unison to snatch fish, dive to retrieve tourists' wristwatches, dance and wiggle on their tails, and

Sometimes it's worth getting out of the water on Paradise Island.

squawk-talk to their handler. After that, in a nearby pool, sea turtles, baby sharks, small barracuda and dozens of beautiful tropical fish are fed as you watch at close quarters.

During the day, walking the shaded roads and paths of Paradise Island is pleasant. Along some dirt tracks you may see "treasure holes," where people are said to have dug even recently in hopes of finding old pirate booty. You may also be shown spots where some of the action in the James Bond movie *Thunderball* was filmed.

Toward the eastern end of the island are the unexpected

Versailles Gardens with statuary adorning a long row of manicured terraces, and the French Cloister, built in Montréjeau near Lourdes, France, by Augustinian monks in the 14th century and shipped here in pieces for reconstruction 600 years later.

An inexpensive bus keeps a somewhat informal schedule from early morning until past midnight, linking Paradise Island's hotels, casino complex, ferry dock and golf course.

Around the Island

Exploring by rented car, motorscooter or guided tour, you'll be struck by the economic contrasts on New Providence. Most of the population lives "over the hill" in crowded and modest communities which began as slave settlements, south of the ridge overlooking Nassau town. Here you'll see pastel clapboard houses with shutters askew, tiny fruit and vegetable markets set up in front yards or

on porches, legions of small children at open-windowed kindergartens and primary schools. "We got a bar for every church," a resident may tell you. There's a profusion of bougainvillea (the Bahamas boasts at least five shades: deep purple, lavender, scarlet, white, orange) in this area, just as there is in such "rich man's" districts as Prospect Ridge and Eastern Road.

West of Nassau there's no missing the gray stone ramparts of **Fort Charlotte** where generations of Nassauvians have sought shelter during hurricanes. Built by Lord Dunmore in 1787–89 and named after the consort of George III, this is the largest fort in the Bahamas. (The only shots ever fired from it were in 1976 to return a Bicentennial U.S. salute from three American warships in the harbor.) Tourists are escorted into the dungeon which never held prisoners but today houses a mock-up of a torture chamber complete with stretching rack. While entry is free, "gratuities are permissible" for the fort's amusing guides.

In the same area, marching flamingoes are the remarkable attraction at **Ardastra Garden.** About two dozen of the gangling pink birds parade at quick step, run, reverse, turn right, and even seem to squawk in unison to a trainer's commands. They also encircle tourists posing for pictures. It takes 14 months to train young flamingoes selected from the nature preserve on Inagua island to do all this. Some of them have been performing for nearly 20 years. You'll also see peacocks, a crocodile and an

Unlikely extravaganza: no guessing the cost of Versailles Gardens. **31**

iguana around these pleasant gardens.

The much larger **Nassau Botanical Gardens** display a great variety of carefully kept tropical flowers and plants covering 18 hillside acres beneath Fort Charlotte.

There's an exotic panoply of sea life on view at **Coral World,** an underwater observatory on Silver Cay. Here you'll find more of those flapping flamingoes you saw at the Ardastra Garden, elegantly gliding sea rays and giant turtles, not to mention fish of every shape, size and color found in the Caribbean, including some fearsome sea

predators. You can handle the merchandise if you want to: should petting a shark seem too risky, maybe you'll settle for cuddling a sea urchin. The establishment offers water sports and boasts a private beach, restaurant and gift shops. You can even make a hit with friends at home by sending off a postcard from the only underwater post office in existence.

Farther west past the CABLE BEACH resort strip you'll come to some roadside caves said locally to have been the haunt of both smugglers and ghosts. They're near the appealing little settlement of GAMBIER which features

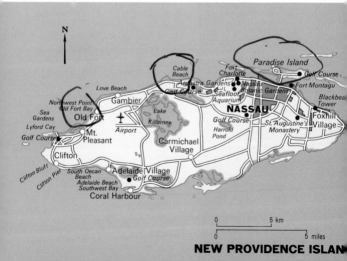

NEW PROVIDENCE ISLAND

colored wooden-slat houses, dozens of beaming children, scratching chickens, snoozing dogs, and a few ruined stone slave huts. Sunbathers at picturesque LOVE BEACH watch nearby jetliners low overhead coming in to land at Nassau International Airport.

A better beach, probably the finest on New Providence, is past Northwest Point at **Old Fort Bay.** This gentle arc of soft sand is backed by dense tropical foliage in which stand the remains of an old fort, now part of a private residence. From here the coastal road passes LYFORD CAY, an exclusive residential and yachting preserve to which the public is not admitted.

Farther around the southwestern tip of the island in the Clifton area you'll pass overgrown ruins of an old settlement. Just off the road here, at an unmarked spot locals can show you, is a large rocky grotto. It's speculated that this was a "slave pit"; you can climb down in to investigate. Near CLIFTON PIER there are more ruins, including a rather well-preserved two-storey plantation great house. Unusually, there are considerable cliffs along the shore here. A set of stone steps leading down toward the sea may date back to early pirate days, or the slave era—nobody knows for certain.

There are ruins of another plantation house near the 15th green of the South Ocean Beach golf course, where there's also an "ocean hole." The islands have many of these inland holes, often quarrylike in appearance, in which the water level rises and falls with the tides.

Small, isolated and charmingly unspoiled, **Adelaide Village** on Southwest Bay dates back to 1832 when it was settled by slaves freed from ships stopped by the Royal Navy. A prominent sign announces the next "Be Healed Revival Meeting." Friendly villagers are pleased to chat for as long as a visitor wishes. Adelaide's few dozen humble wooden houses are painted various unlikely colors. You may see a baby with black cloth wrapped around one wrist. "That's to render off evil," the mother explains. Out here, Nassau town and the 20th century seem very remote.

The elaborate CORAL HARBOUR resort and residential area with striking palm-lined avenues has been relatively quiet in recent years, though prospects seem good for a revival of marina and watersport tourism. Elsewhere along **33**

Near Potters Cay you'll see a mini-mountain of discarded conch shells.

the south coast there is little of sightseeing interest.

In the eastern section of the island, FOXHILL VILLAGE is another sleepy old wooden house settlement (which livens up dramatically on weekends with "Jump 'n Dance" at local clubs). You'll see a "laundry mat" or two and a mini police station near the huge central silk cotton tree. This has always been fruit territory and in summer Nassauvians drive out to buy fresh mangoes, tamarinds, and sapodillas from Foxhill's roadside stands.

Appropriately perched on a hillock overlooking the eastern approach to Nassau harbor is **Blackbeard's Tower,** popularly supposed to be a lookout built by the 17th-century pirate chief. It's reasonably intact, and climbing the few steps rewards you with a good **view** out over coco plum, coconut palm and sapodilla trees to the sea. The tower is up a short path off Eastern Road, which meanders back toward town past scores of lovely residences. Fort Montagu, the island's oldest and smallest fort, saw considerable action after its construction in 1741 but it's hardly worth visiting.

Past the row of busy north-shore marinas, you reach proud Paradise Island bridge, spanning the channel with one odd hump. Beneath the bridge is some of the best fun Nassau has to offer. This is **Potters Cay,** where throughout the day (mornings are best), little fishing boats tie up with conch, turtle, grouper and snapper which are snapped up by local householders and res-

taurateurs. There may be some good-natured bargaining, though a non-Bahamian will have difficulty deciphering the dialect. Something worth watching or photographing is always going on under the bridge on what could be the smallest yet most important cay in the Bahamas. Major events are arrivals and departures of mail boats, which carry all kinds of cargo and passengers between Nassau and the Family Islands.

Water Excursions

If you're not continuing on to the Family Islands, you'll want to take at least one of the many water tours offered to Nassau/Paradise visitors. The trips last as little as an hour, as long as a day. Most popular are glass-bottom boat rides to the **"Sea Gardens,"** coral reef clusters off the eastern end of Paradise Island. The motor launches depart frequently from Prince George Wharf downtown, less often from quays at **35**

Paradise Island. Through the glass you'll almost certainly see a few small sharks and stingrays as well as schools of striped sergeant majors, dazzling blue and black tangs and rainbow fish, groupers, yellowtail and gray snappers. Occasionally a good-sized barracuda may appear, or a sea turtle. Boatmen regularly feed fish, which is why they flock up to your boat. Fishing and snorkeling are forbidden here.

Longer, wetter and even more rewarding are excursions to snorkeling and diving reefs at nearby cays and islets. **Sandy Cay,** variously nicknamed Treasure Island or Honeymoon

Impatience is best swallowed—the boats depart only with a full load.

Island, is possibly the most photographed speck of sand and palm trees in the Commonwealth. It has been owned by the same family since 1870 when it was bought at auction for one pound sterling. A 45-minute scenic cruise takes you to Sandy Cay, 6 nautical miles northeast of Rawson Square, where you can swim, snorkel, laze, count the (150) palm trees, play with hundreds of little curly-tailed San Salvador lizards, or look for the couple of resident iguanas.

Grand Bahama

The flat, 65-mile-long northern island of Grand Bahama, with its sunshine, palm beaches and sparkling seas, is the consummate vacation island as programmed in the late 20th century.

Freeport/Lucaya

If Grand Bahama island is typical of the Bahamas, the surprising commercial and resort center of Freeport/Lucaya certainly is not. Despite English place names and tours by red London double-deck bus, basic Bahamian local color is in short supply here. The atmosphere is more palpably American than anywhere else in the Commonwealth—not unexpectedly, since it was a Norfolk Virginia financier, Wallace Groves, who conceived and set in motion the "Freeport miracle" in 1955.* Most of the island's 32,000 residents live in this city—or at the West End settlement some 25 miles away. Smooth highways—neatly landscaped, clearly signpost-

*Under the Hawksbill Creek agreement of that year, a deep-water harbor was decided upon along with the tax- and duty-free port. Tourism began to boom when the first casino opened in 1964.

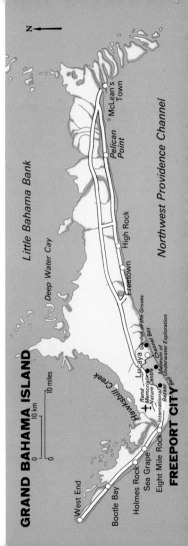

ed and even at times divided—connect modern hotels with golf courses, marinas, a shopping and gambling complex.

Freeport's **International Bazaar,** an unusual mixture of architecture and offerings from various parts of the world, is the city's major sightseeing attraction, and worth wandering through even if you're not buying from any of the scores of shops. Built in 1967, it was the work of a Hollywood set designer. Within the Bazaar's 10 acres is a Ministry of Tourism information centre. Close by are the huge **Bahamas Princess Casino** with its Moorish façade, and the island's main straw market where ladies with broad beams are used to posing for photographers. Major Freeport hotels and golf courses are also in the area.

The atmosphere is more authentically Bahamian at the native fruit and vegetable market, an all-weather cluster of family stalls in Churchill Square, and at the occasional fairs, parades and "jumpin'" religious events.

Starting a few miles east of Freeport's central attractions, the sprawling **Lucaya** resort area features beachfront and marina hotels, the island's best golf courses and several sightseeing possibilities.

"Please do not touch the plants—many are poisonous," says the entrance sign at the **Garden of the Groves.** But that's the only jarring note in these thoroughly delightful 11 acres of tropical flora, man-made waterfalls and ponds. Lizards scamper as you stroll among the 10,000 plants and trees. The tranquil gardens, which honor Freeport's founder, are open daily without charge.

From BELL CHANNEL BAY, wind conditions permitting, what's billed as the world's largest **glass-bottom boat** takes tourists over coral gardens and along Grand Bahama's deep reef. Sharks, barracudas, stingrays and other large creatures are usually seen. A diver feeds fish for photographers poised on the dry side of the glass. Boat tours are also available for snorkeling and fishing.

Undersea buffs might enjoy the **Museum of Underwater Exploration** at the Underwater Explorers Society in the same inlet. Aside from various items brought up by divers, some early underwater gear, including primitive-looking cameras and masks, is displayed.

Around the diving facilities in the area, you'll hear about the million or more dollars

worth of Spanish pieces-of-eight found offshore from Lucaya in 1964. The shallow site, long since stripped of its gold, is nicknamed Treasure Reef.

To the north, on East Settlers Way, the 100-acre **Rand Memorial Nature Centre** offers 90-minute guided walks with a

Freeport sightseers retreat from the heat at Garden of the Groves.

naturalist through a protected Bahamian forest, and the chance to photograph flamingoes and other uncommon birds.

39

Heading West

For the tourist, the most interesting thing about HAWKSBILL CREEK is that conch fishermen from as far away as Abaco bring their boats into the creek mouth and sell their catch. At the informal waterside market, you'll see mountains of discarded conch shells.

At the settlement of EIGHT MILE ROCK, which is strung out along a good highway, guided tours stop at a Bahamian rarity, a perfume factory,

West End resort pool is worlds apart from modest village nearby.

formerly a Baptist church. You can watch oils from around the world being mixed and bottled as various fragrances. Mysteriously, a number of old cannonballs have been found in this area recently, though not even pirates were supposed to have lived on Grand Bahama until the 1840s.

Signs make good reading along the road, as you pass such places as SEA GRAPE, DEADMAN'S REEF and BOTTLE BAY. Near HOLMES ROCK a small commercial nursery called Hydro Flora Gardens offers a tour and lecture on tropical plants grown without soil.

West End, sadly, isn't what it used to be. Searching the sleepy seaside village, you'll find only the scantiest traces of the bad old days of Prohibition when merchants and rum runners here made fortunes smuggling liquor into the United States. A few old-timers recall the bootlegging boom days when, for example, a boat owned by Al Capone was loaded with booze here. In the "gin clear" water just offshore in front of the aged Star Hotel landmark and the so-called Old Factory, you'll see some concrete slabs of Prohibition-era piers and bits of old iron rails used to roll contraband down to waiting boats. In this oldest Grand Bahama settlement there are six churches and over 20 bars or clubs, mostly small wooden affairs. West End's 5,000 inhabitants don't benefit as much as they'd like from a large, self-sustaining tourist hotel complex which dominates the area. From here you can go on deep-sea fishing and scuba diving excursions.

Out East

Tourists won't normally find it convenient to take the bus which goes most days between Freeport and the eastern end of the island. By taxi or rented car, it's a long drive on a road which deteriorates dramatically beyond the U.S. Air Force missile tracking installations around HIGH ROCK. From the road you'll see impressive radar dishes and antennae, but stern signs prohibit closer inspection. On this trip you parallel the majority of Grand Bahama's advertised 60 miles of beaches, mostly long windswept stretches frequented only by birds and crabs. Tiny PELICAN POINT is a tidy, friendly roadside settlement where the center of all things is the Baptist church.

McLean's Town, metropolis of the east end, has about 250 inhabitants who live in pastel **41**

wooden houses. Here, too, almost everyone attends every service at the Baptist church. This settlement is unusual in that the majority of the women go out fishing for a living, as do the menfolk. They bring in snapper, grouper, conch, porgy and crawfish. A bit shy at first, villagers are genuinely pleased to welcome strangers—in the fashion of Family-Islanders around the Bahamas. They're particularly happy to tell you about the town's biggest event of the year, the Conch Cracking Contest held on Discovery Day, October 12, when huge crowds turn up to watch competitors from as far afield as Bimini crack, empty and clean up to 25 conchs in less than three minutes.

Otherwise, nothing much happens in McLean's Town. But older folks still recall a gigantic black whale which washed ashore here in 1940. They say it was much more than 100 feet long.

At a fishing camp on nearby DEEP WATER CAY, you'll hear other sea sagas from the regulars. There's very good bonefishing in the shallows among the east end mangroves, and collecting seashells (shelling) can be superb along such beaches as CRABBIN BAY and **42** JOHN DAVIS.

The Family Islands

The Bahamas archipelago is usually considered to consist of three elements: New Providence, Grand Bahama, and all the rest—referred to collectively as the "Out Islands" (or Family Islands, as official nomenclature has it).

Many of these most beautiful spots are uninhabited, seen fleetingly from an airplane and visited only by native fishermen or fortunate travelers aboard yachts. Other islands and cays, notably far south in the archipelago, are sparsely settled, with few or no tourist facilities.* While the vast majority of remote Bahamian islands will probably remain forever undisturbed, there are more than enough which are reasonably accessible to satisfy any escapist.

On a normal vacation, you could not expect to see more than a few of these far-flung Family Islands. Scheduled air and sea services are not very satisfactory; small plane charters are available but expensive. This makes island hopping in the Bahamas somewhat

---

* This is true, for example, of the salt-producing island of Inagua where perhaps 20,000 West Indian flamingos nest in a large, tranquil preserve.

difficult. With few flights *between* Family Islands, you must often return to Nassau or Florida and then fly back out to another island. A limited number of one-day excursions to Family Islands from Nassau are available.

Some mail boats from Nassau touch several islands on their runs; they're fun if you're adventurous, and the price is right, but they're slow and not always reliable (see p. 125). Certain cruise-ships from Florida ports may stop at lesser islands as well as Nassau and Freeport.

This book describes the nine most interesting and most frequented Family Islands or clusters, roughly clockwise from Nassau. They vary greatly. But even those with de luxe resorts are worlds apart from the sophistication of Nassau and Freeport.

Abaco

Many vacationers will find nothing better in all the Bahamas than this long, arching archipelago. Revolutionary War loyalists fleeing the New York, Bermuda and Carolina colonies two centuries ago knew a good island when they landed on one and today the descendants of these settlers and their slaves are proud of their heritage and convinced this is the finest possible place to live. When you see the settlements of Hope Town and New Plymouth, you may agree.

Stretching for some 130 miles, the Abaco group consists of "mainland" Little and Great Abaco with an attendant string of cays and islets. Total population is about 9,000. There are excellent tourist facilities, but only at a handful of spots. If you possibly can, visit by boat: the sailing is glorious on Abaco's "inland sea" of some 1,000 protected square miles. Water taxis run to some of the best diving and snorkeling sites. Wild boar are still hunted in the Abaco bush, but the celebrated wild horses descended from Cuban imports early this century have almost all died out.

At the top of the Abaco chain, tiny **Walker's Cay** is a renowned sports fishing resort which is also within easy reach of some exciting underwater sights for divers and snorkelers. Annual billfishing tournaments here attract swarms of anglers. This is the northernmost piece of Bahamian territory and is reached by small plane from Florida, Grand Bahama or Nassau.

Green Turtle Cay is one of the most appealing hideaways **43**

in the Bahamas. Half a dozen places to stay are scattered around the deeply indented coastline of this slightly hilly 3-mile-long island. Beaches are lonely and lovely. The 450 residents get around on foot or by boat rather than in cars.

The only settlement, **New Plymouth,** is an unlikely flashback to traditional New England but with palm trees. Trim and brightly painted wooden homes have picket fences and blooming flowers.

For a fascinating look at Abaconian history since the first loyalists arrived here in 1783, don't miss the **Albert Lowe Museum** housed in a restored two-storey house built 150 years ago. The Lowe family has led the effort to preserve New Plymouth's colonial era atmosphere. Among other exhibits, the museum possesses a 175-year-old black cast-iron stove from Troy, New York, complete with its original brass pokers and trim. You'll also see

Albert Lowe's magnificent redwood model of a four-mast schooner is memorable exhibit at his museum.

a 19th-century bedroom, early harpoons for hunting shark and sea turtles, and a wonderful 50-year-old telephone switchboard.

Nowadays green turtles are rare on Green Turtle Cay, but they're still caught at deserted creeks and cays nearby, so that beloved steamed or "stew turtle" continues to appear on menus. Aside from tourism, the islanders' main source of income is from the export of crawfish tails to the United States.

A speedy family ferry service brings visitors the 2½ miles out to the cay from a sleepy dock on **Great Abaco** close to the Treasure Cay International Airport. Here, as throughout the Abacos, CB radio is used for everything from ordering a taxi to calling for help in **45** an emergency. Arriving from Florida or Nassau, you encounter a large sign of welcome to northern Abaco "where your sufficiencies will be surfancified".

The airport also serves the extensive **Treasure Cay** resort complex on a nearby peninsula of Great Abaco, which offers golf, tennis, fishing, boating and wetter water sports. Despite the name, there's no suggestion of any pirate gold hidden, hereabouts.

The best snorkeling in this area is over a reef off BAKER'S POINT at the northwestern tip of Great Guana Cay where you should spot barracuda, trigger fish, stingrays, jacks and some nurse sharks.

Great Guana Cay, longest offshore island in the Abacos, is about as far out in the Bahamas as you can get and still have some resort conveniences. Non-yachting visitors arrive by water taxi from Marsh Harbour where there's an airport. Along the ocean side of Great Guana, beachcombers will find seven uninterrupted miles of white sand. There are no roads or motor vehicles on the cay. In the absence of iguanas, lively lizards do their best. (The Commonwealth has two islands called Great Guana Cay and five called Guana Cay. Iguanas, prized eating by generations of Bahamians, are nowadays almost impossible to find.)

With practically no competition, shelling and fishing can be outstanding on this island. Underwater photographers and snorkelers will appreciate the offshore reefs. In Guana Cay settlement near the only hotel and harbor, some of the island's six dozen natives live in simple old New England style houses. There's a bit of fishing, farming and woodworking. You'll see the church, a provision store or two, the one-room schoolhouse and the little wooden telephone office which functions for about four hours a day.

Scotland Cay, which some locals feel is the most beautiful island in the Abacos, is privately owned by European and North American winter residents.

Immediately to the southeast is the **Fowl Cay Underwater Park,** with some of the finest snorkeling and diving in the Bahamas. No fishing or removing of coral is permitted. In brilliantly clear water no more than 18 feet deep, you'll see a tremendous selection of fish and turtles among superior corals.

Man-O-War Cay, named
after the frigate bird and not
a battleship, still builds some
of the wooden runabouts and
dinghies for which its boat-
yards have long been famous.
You'll marvel at them when
you're ferried around this
central part of the Abacos.
Man-O-War is unusual as it

*Independent, hard-working, proud,
Man-O-War looks after its own.*

has always been a dry cay (no
liquor or beer sold any-
where); its few hundred inhabitants are all either loyalist descendants or Americans
and its obvious industrious-

ness has brought impressive prosperity; its real estate is said to be the most expensive in the Bahamas. Transport is by bicycle or golf cart. The island, a model of cleanliness, has no jail and no police. About 90 per cent of the locals attend one of the two churches, and just about every inhabitant sat, from 1st to 11th grade, on benches you'll see at the yellow-and-white wooden school. Man-O-War has no hotels, but there are about 20 cottages for rent with easy access to a good Atlantic beach and the busy harbor. Along the waterfront, ask to see the rib, backbone and jawbone of a 22-foot killer whale which was washed onto the cay years ago. Offshore, sport fishermen bring in good-sized marlin.

Four miles across the channel on the Abaco mainland is **Marsh Harbour,** go-ahead hub of the Abacos and the third largest town in the Bahamas (pop. 3,500). Visitors arrive at a briskly efficient little airport or at friendly marinas, and are taken care of with the aid of omnipresent CB radios. Boating is big business. A more prominent landmark is a large turreted, castle-like house, described as "bilious green"

by locals, built by an American science professor turned island medical doctor and author. Guests report that one turret has a bathtub another a toilet.

The nearby settlements of DUNDAS TOWN and MURPHY TOWN are more colorful, less affluent, but just as friendly. You'll find beaches for good shelling south of Marsh Harbour at CASUARINA POINT and BAHAMA PALM SHORES where there is also fine bonefishing. Abaco's best shelling, though, is said to be along the beach at SANDY POINT in the far southwest.

Hope Town, on Elbow Cay three miles across the water from Marsh Harbour, is probably the most charming spot in the Bahamas. Yachts at anchor clutter the nearly circular harbor beneath a candy-striped lighthouse few photographers can resist. The neat little village of wooden cottages reminds American visitors of Nantucket or other New England seaside points. The post office, painted green

Reliable Hope Town lighthouse cut dubious spoils of wrecking trade.

and white, perches above the unused jailhouse. Along that lane in a small century-old house is the **Wyannie Malone Historical Museum,** exhibiting what Hope Towners have been able to discover about their roots. Most of the village's residents today, and many other Bahamians, trace their ancestry to the widow Malone, who came here from Charleston, South Carolina with her four children about 1785. In the museum you'll learn about sponging, wrecking, timbering, shipbuilding, hurricanes and other aspects of Abaconian life.

There are places to stay at Hope Town and in a few other spots on this slender, ridged island. Good beach lines much of Elbow Cay's Atlantic shore, sheltered by continuous reef which branches in close to shore at some spots for easy snorkeling. You'll have even better undersea viewing off Sandy Cay in **Pelican Cay National Park,** Abaco's second undersea preserve, a short boat trip south of Elbow Cay. Among the expert admirers of this teeming coral reef is Jacques Cousteau. *Note:* Water taxis can be summoned by CB radio from Man-O-War Cay to get to the other islands in the area.

Eleuthera

Long, slender and slightly rolling, Eleuthera—pronounced Eloothra—and its offshore satellites have more tourist facilities than anywhere else in the Family Islands. Three airports—North Eleuthera, mid-island Governor's Harbour and Rock Sound in the south—serve resorts spread widely over 100 miles. The "Queen's Highway," particularly well paved in central Eleuthera, makes it feasible to explore from north to south by rented car or by taxi with the driver acting as guide.

Modern Bahamian history began on this island in 1648 when the Eleutherian Adventurers landed and founded their shaky colony, now hailed as probably the western world's first modern democracy. Aside from history, fine beaches and picturesque settlements, Eleuthera offers pineapple rum, which you may well consider the tastiest item produced in the Bahamas.

Touring from the north, **Spanish Wells,** a fascinating settlement on small ST. GEORGE'S CAY, boasts the most proficient fishermen in the country. About a dozen boats go out for crawfish, grouper, yellowtail snapper, turtle and conch, with the considerable proceeds from this and farming going into very attractive houses. Many have manicured lawns of Bermuda grass and meticulously maintained evergreens. The best-known local product is the very wide-brimmed "Spanish Wells straw hat". The village is as clean as any in the Bahamas. Its narrow waterfront with marina facilities resembles certain small Mediterranean fishing ports.

Most of Spanish Wells' 1,200 residents are descendants of Eleutherian Adventurers or loyalists, and they've kept largely to themselves over the centuries though in recent years a few black Bahamians have also become residents. The settlement retains its original name but today gets its water by pipe from the nearby main island instead of from the wells Spanish seamen used to prize here. Tourists appreciate the cay's good stretch of white sand beach and many miles of offshore reef. Spanish Wells marine pilots, who may double as sport fishing guides, are invaluable for boaters in this potentially hazardous area.

Ask a local citizen why Spanish Wells is so desirable, and you may hear: "Best is the quiet. When we lay down here nights, we don't got no worries."

From North Eleuthera airport it's about half an hour by taxi and ferry to Spanish Wells.

Despite the long-standing fresh water problem, charming old **Harbour Island** generates enormous enthusiasm among visitors and residents. Its publicized 3-mile pink beach, backed by sea grapes, low shrubs and occasional palm stands, makes a marvelous early morning walk. The sand, of coral pulverized over millennia by the ocean, is unquestionably pale pink. It's also amazingly soft. If you like it, you can buy a bottle to take home.

DUNMORE TOWN is relaxed and quaint with restored stately residences providing traces of elegance. It was named after Lord Dunmore, who spent summers here when he wasn't building forts in Nassau. For some time this was a prosperous shipbuilding center and the country's second largest town. When you see the sleepy waterfront today, that may seem hard to believe. Cruising, fishing and diving excursions leave from the harbor. Wandering around (you can stroll over the entire island in a few hours), you'll find the "Loyalist Cottage, 1797", "Miss Lena's Cotton Tree House", eight churches, tidy little wooden **51** homes including one painted peach color with bright lavender shutters and doors, chickens among weather-scarred tombstones in a simple cemetery, and everywhere droves of laughing, barefooted children. Brilanders, as they call themselves, wave at strangers and friends from their front porches. High-rise buildings are forbidden. After dark there's as much church music as disco beat.

Harbour Island is a 5-minute, inexpensive motor-launch ride from a point on the main island close to North Eleuthera's airport.

Tradition has it that after being shipwrecked, those first Puritan adventurers sheltered

Blooming at Cape Eleuthera resort complex and throughout the Bahamas, the hibiscus (right) is among the most beautiful flowers.

for a while in **Preacher's Cave,** which you can visit in Eleuthera's far north. Hereabouts are deserted beaches with good close-to-shore snorkeling such as Bain Bay and Ridley Head. Your taxi guide in this area may sing you homemade hymns between descriptions of island sights.

Smiles prevail at the sleepy seaside farming settlement of Bluff, which is proud of its tiny pink public school and the straw work of its women.

Current, with little more than 100 natives and a few American winter residents, is named after the strong ocean flow through the offshore cut which provides a dramatic dive for scuba vacationers here.

The famed **Glass Window** was a natural arched hole through the island at a point where Eleuthera narrows to a rocky ridge just 80 feet wide. It collapsed in hurricane waves and today you pass over the still dramatic gap from north to

The best panorama for Governor's Harbour sunsets is from atop the communications transmitter ridge.

central Eleuthera on a bridge. In the ocean off Glass Window is a coral reef called the Plateau, accessible by boat from Harbour Island or Whale Point, which some scuba divers call the "ultimate underwater experience". Just south on the island you'll see huge rocks which are nicknamed Cow and Bull because wind whistling around them causes a mooing sound. Nearby GOULDING CAY beach is shaded by palm and casuarina trees.

The friendliness of **Gregory Town,** a pretty hillside settlement overlooking a small semicircular cove in central Eleuthera, is what the Out Islands are all about. Any of the few hundred gentle villagers may swamp you with their welcome. You'll find them convinced that the pineapples grown in the red clay soil here are the softest, sweetest and juiciest in the world. (Hawaiian pineapples, you're assured, are tarter and stringier.) This is where Eleuthera pineapple rum is made. There's also a bakery which is very hard to resist. Gregory Town, named after the first English governor, is one of the oldest Bahamian settlements. Some of the tourists who arrive today are young Americans who spend their days at **Surfer's Beach,** or Twin Silos Beach, riding what has been called the "second best wave in the world".

A mile south, the **Budho caves** have huge stalagmites and stalactites, and bats in a conelike ceiling hole. Extending for half a mile to a sub-surface depth of 87 feet, the caverns are best seen with a guide from the marina at Hatchet Bay. He'll also direct you to **"Shark Hole"** on the Atlantic side beneath a 15-foot-high cliff. In late afternoon poultry leftovers from a large government farm here are dumped into the sea, attracting dozens of sharks of various types. You'll see the show well only on calm days. In SWEETINGS POND on the property of the poultry farm, there's unusual sea life including huge turtles which inspire local monster legends. At HATCHET BAY, rental cars and helpful local information are available, and taxis serve the Governor's Harbour airport.

Rising above a protected bay enclosed by Cupid's Cay, the once-flourishing town of **Governor's Harbour** is a photographer's favorite. Today Governor's Harbour is quiet and modest, some of its buildings as much as 150 years old and showing their age. Many of the 800 inhabitants are also old-timers: few people have emigrated from the town. You'll hear that the Bahamas' first turtle meat cannery was here, which seems to count locally much more than the fact that this was an original Eleutherian Adventurer settlement. CUPID'S CAY, perhaps the oldest settlement with the oldest houses in the Bahamas, has deteriorated and is best seen from afar.

Along the Atlantic side of the island opposite Governor's **55**

Harbour run 12 miles of partly pink, powdery beach, accessible from a large vacation club complex.

The drowsy hamlet of NORTH PALMETTO POINT features one of the best "lazy trees" in the Bahamas. This huge old gray-trunked silk cotton tree shades the casual main square where idlers idle amid chickens, goats and children in front of the venerable (1916) "Burial Society Hall".

Swank **Windmere Island,** just offshore beyond a mangrove channel in southern Eleuthera, is worth visiting for its away-from-it-all driftwood beach and beautifully kept gardens, even if you don't join the tennis buffs who flock here. The palms, bougainvillea and casuarinas are memorable. Bird-watching can be excellent.

Derelict fishing boats tell of the past in TARPUM BAY with its faded pastel shacks among hulks of churches and shuttered buildings. In contrast, a bit farther south **Rock Sound** thrives, with a modern shopping center and freshly painted picket fences. You'll probably have to ask directions to the **"Ocean Hole",** which is east of the town center. It may be the best and most accessible of such attractions in the Baha-

mas. Gliding around the crystal green water of a large quarry-like tidal pond are all kinds of tropical fish eager to accept your handout. A rock ledge allows very close-up viewing or camera work. Divers have been unable to find the hole's bottom.

On the ocean side of the island below Rock Sound, the **Cotton Bay** palm tree and white sand beach with a coral reef about a mile offshore is not far from perfection. The noted seaside golf course here is a particular draw, and bonefish are said to haunt nearby shallows. There are marina facilities across the island at DAVIS HARBOUR and in a large resort complex at POWELL POINT.

In the rarely visited extreme south of Eleuthera, long strips of tan sand line the shores, with extensive close-in reefs promising virgin snorkeling, diving and fishing.

Cat Island

Progress hasn't much troubled this remote island of wide open beaches, deep creeks and scenic hills, high by Bahamian standards. Getting there may not be half the fun: Cat Island has been plagued by problems with scheduled air transportation into modest New Bight airfield which serves the handful of resort hotels. If Bahamasair is operating from Nassau, it's about an hour's flight of spectacular beauty over some of the Exuma Cays and southern Eleuthera, and you'll be effusively welcomed by barefoot Cat Islanders. Otherwise, small planes land at airstrips in the deep south and far north, or there's always the mail boat.

Disregarding the consensus of historians, many Cat Islanders remain convinced that Columbus first landed here, rather than on nearby San Salvador. They're not so certain why their island has its name, but the best explanation seems to be that it commemorates an English sea captain called Catt, the second "t" dropped some time in the past.

Most tourist interest centers on Cat Island's bootshaped south. The gently curving beach at **Fernandez Bay** is among the most beautiful in the Bahamas. It's shorter than the exposed 3-mile beach at **Old Bight,** also greatly admired. Up north, they insist that **Pigeon Cay's** beach with old cedar trees near BENNETT'S HARBOUR tops them all. (These strands are all on the protected, Exuma Sound side of the island where watersports and

shelling are generally better.) Along the Atlantic coast there are literally dozens of miles of deserted, windblown beach. You may be able to rent a horse for speedy, long-distance beachcombing. Apart from hotel transportation, the island, at the time of writing, has only one rental car.

Not far from the NEW BIGHT settlement is the highest point in the Bahamas, **Mount Alvernia,** which rises all of 206 feet above sea level. By car over a rough track you can get within an easy 15-minute walk of the summit. Along the rocky upward path are cement reliefs of the Stations of the Cross. At the top is a clean mini-hermitage built of white stone by locally famous Father Jerome, an Anglican missionary turned Roman Catholic. He died at 80 in 1956 after erecting various Out Island churches and is buried in a small hilltop cave. His retreat here commands a grand **view** over both Cat Island coasts.

The island's other celebrity, actor Sidney Poitier, was born in ARTHUR'S TOWN in the far north. His relatives now live around New Bight. It's a rare Cat Islander who hasn't seen Sidney's movies.

All over the countryside you'll notice low stone "slave **57** walls" which marked off plantations. Farming is still a major occupation among the 3,000 Cat Islanders. It's claimed local sugarloaf pineapples are just as sweet as Eleuthera's.

Natives believe that seven or eight old ships wrecked in the offshore shoals have still to be located, but although treasure hunters have exhaustively explored the caves in the deep south, only one cache of pirate gold has been found—buried beneath a large tomb near the friendly little southern settlement of BAIN'S TOWN.

Islanders will cheerfully tell you about their bush medicines used for all manner of aches and internal disorders. They're less forthcoming about *obeah*, minor witchcraft rituals still practised by some older folks on this and other Bahamian islands.

A Cat Island sight always pointed out to visitors is a former three-headed **coconut palm tree** about a mile outside Arthur's Town (a storm recently reduced it to two heads). This is thought to be the only such palm tree in the world.

One of the Bahamas' finest **views** over coast and reef-studded sea is from the hilly northwestern tip of Cat Island, a walk of perhaps 3 miles beyond ORANGE CREEK.

San Salvador

Somewhere on this sleepy, unassuming island is where it all began. Around the shoreline you'll find several separate monuments purporting to mark the site of Columbus' landing and "discovery of America." No one will ever know, of course, but theorizing is bound to increase as the 500th anniversary of the great day (in 1992) gets closer.

San Salvador's claim to historic fame hasn't ever done much for this far out, sparsely populated, lake-littered island. But recently it has burst onto the world tourism map as an outstanding scuba diving location (see p. 115). The undersea spectacle, not yet fully explored, draws an ever-growing number of visitors. They arrive at a good airstrip, one legacy of a mostly abandoned U.S. military presence on San Salvador. The mail boat takes about two days from Nassau, nearly 200 miles to the northeast.

Cockburn Town, the principal settlement, has the island's one public telephone, a jail house with the door falling

Columbus could hardly be blamed for choosing this beach for his first landing in the New World.

off, and next to a seaside cemetery a fine almond "lazy tree" more than 100 years old. The Catholic church, one of about a dozen well attended churches on San Salvador, sports a freshly painted, pale yellow and vaguely feminine representation of Columbus.

Just south of town on **Fernandez Bay,** a simple stone and cement slab carries the legend: "Christopher Columbus made the first recorded landing in the New World on this beach Oct. 12, 1492. Yawl Heloise, Feb. 25, 1951." The crew of this vessel erected the marker on the sea grape and palm tree beach after completing an around-the-world voyage.

A few minutes farther south, on the beach at **Long Bay** (named either after the longboat in which Columbus came ashore or after the broad expanse of water here), is the best known monument. This is a 9-foot high whitewashed cross, endlessly photographed, with the sign: "On or near this spot Christopher Columbus landed on the 12th October 1492," attributing the site to researches made by the famed historian Samuel Eliot Morison. Nearby stands an impressive metal structure erected by Mexicans to hold the Olympic flame which passed through here from Greece en route to the Mexico City games in 1968.

In the extreme southwest near SANDY POINT you'll see limestone ridges and caverns. Most interesting is so-called Dripping Rock cave where formidable soldier crabs guard an old well. Offshore in nearby **French Bay** is perhaps the best scuba diving in the Bahamas. Inshore snorkeling and shelling are also superior here.

A short drive away are ruins of a loyalist plantation, among the largest of the former slave estates scattered around San Salvador. This is known as **Watling's Castle,** after a noted pirate who operated from the island. Until about 50 years ago, San Salvador was called Watling's Island.

An extended tour by minibus will take you along the southern road past some high rocky coastal scenery unusual in the Bahamas. From SANDY HOOK at beautiful **Snow Bay** or from the mouth of PIGEON CREEK you'll see three offshore islets, Low, Middle and High Cay, and a gray boat-shaped rock named… Boat Rock. It's suggested that High Cay, which is white from exposure to the ocean, was the "head of sand" Columbus' lookout first spotted after their long Atlantic crossing. Up the rough and generally uninteresting east coast road, you'll pass more plantation ruins and the site of an archaeological dig which has yielded some pre-Columbian items.

To reach another Columbus monument, a beige marble globe on gray stone, you walk about 2 miles from EAST BEACH along the shore of **Crab Cay.** In 1892, on the 400th anniversary, the *Chicago Herald* decided that Columbus first came ashore here on the point of the cay which faces dangerous reefs and Atlantic currents. (It's believed now that in fact, the explorer wisely sailed to the island's protected, leeward side before landing.)

Toward the northeastern point where there's a small U.S. Coast Guard station, the **Dixon Hill Lighthouse** is often visited. Built in 1856 but improved since, it is called the last "hand-operated kerosene-lit lighthouse" in the Bahamas. Every 10 seconds it flashes a beam visible for some 20 miles.

In the northwest, SAND DOLLAR BEACH and BONEFISH BAY live up to their names.

Long Island

Columbus said this was the most beautiful island he'd ever seen in that busy October of 1492.

The resident Indians called it Yuma but the explorer renamed it Fernandina to honor the King of Spain. Later the English measured its 57 rolling miles and decreed it Long Island. It's also narrow—nowhere much more than 4 miles across. Commercial planes fly into two good airfields, at Stella Maris and Deadman's Cay.

Bahamians admire this island for its boatbuilders and fishermen, its annual Salt Pond regatta and, some say, the prettiest girls in the country. Everyone raves about freshly baked bread sticks or "fingers".

Tourism, concentrated in a northern resort complex, focuses on some more of the Bahamas' most exciting diving and snorkeling (see p. 114). Sharing the coastline with rugged cliffs are scores of beaches. The best are probably the lovely 3-mile arc of soft sand at **Calabash Bay** in the far north where there's good reef snorkeling, and the coarse pink sand strip at **Turtle Cove** on the Atlantic near Clarence Town in the south. For both seashells and snorkeling, try **Guana Cay** about 3 miles south of SALT POND, and the long beaches in the far south.

There's one public jitney on Long Island, but exploring is best by rented car. Much of the **61**

north is deserted mangrove creek country, including CO-LUMBUS POINT on a sea-to-sea inlet where the explorer is thought to have landed. Islanders still draw fresh water from Columbus Well near Cape Santa Maria. At the mini-settlement of BURNT GROUND you'll probably see burned ground: dry season scrub fires are common. Some of the island's best bonefishing is in Glenton's Sound. **Gallows Rock** near DEAL'S BEACH has ruins where unruly slaves were kept before being hanged.

Simms is an unhurried old settlement known for its distinctive straw-work, which gracious ladies are delighted to show visitors. The little pale pink building with green shutters here labeled "Her Majesty's Prison" is only occasionally occupied but often photographed. As elsewhere on Long Island, certain householders here paint "X-10" in black over or on their doors to ward off evil spirits. Some believers in *obeah* say spirits can't count past nine and don't know the alphabet up to X, so they'll be discouraged. Others point out that X is the Roman 10, so the sign is simply double insurance. Another precaution is to put turpentine in all four corners of your yard.

In no danger of being spoiled for years if not decades, Calabash Bay at Cape Santa Maria rivals the finest Bahamian and Caribbean beaches.

Near DEADMAN'S CAY and CARTWRIGHT, local people will guide you to dramatic **caves** with unusual rounded stalagmites and Arawak Indian rock drawings. Strong flashlights are necessary.

After passing small pineapple and banana plantations, you'll reach attractive **Clarence Town** with its two large churches, one Anglican, the other Roman Catholic, built by the Cat Island hermit architect Father Jerome. The **Blue Hole** at nearby Turtle Cove, a half-mile walk from the road over rough terrain, is a memorable diving experience and interesting even from the rim. The hole is about 80 yards across and at least 600 feet deep (no plumb line has yet reached the bottom); you'll sometimes see large turtles and tarpon in its waters.

Farther south, tourists may inspect extensive salt flats near HARD BARGAIN, one of three settlements in the Bahamas with that name, suggestive of tough times past.

The Exumas

If you can't sail them, be sure to gaze down when you're flying overhead. This 100-mile string of isles and cays tripping through seas of impossible greens and blues is breathtakingly beautiful. Yachtsmen rhapsodize. The Exumas have a cay for every day of the year, stretching from Hog Cay off Long Island north to Sail Rocks near Nassau. Most are uninhabited, a few still have iguanas. Nobody has counted all the pristine beaches and coves.

Tourist center and principal town of the chain is **George Town** on the largest island,

Disdaining the hard-sell of their Nassau counterparts, George Town's straw ladies leave it to you.

Great Exuma. Commercial flights land at the good airfield here. Don't miss chatting with the devout straw ladies under the grand old fig tree in the heart of the settlement.

Easy-going George Town snaps out of its torpor each April when Bahamians stream in for the Out Island Regatta. This hugely popular three-day competition for working native sailboats fills George Town's broad **Elizabeth Harbour.** A cove in the harbor is named afer Captain Kidd, who used to ide out here with other pirates om English men-of-war.

About 5,000 people live on Great Exuma, spread over ie 45-mile-long island which rows onions, citrus fruits, nangoes and avocado pears eaten with soft grits for breakist, or with peas 'n rice for unch). Much of the land is wned by people called Rolle. hat family name, now comnon around the Bahamas, ame from loyalist plantation wner Lord Rolle of Steventon ho deeded his vast Exuma creage in perpetuity to his reed slaves and their descenants. You'll meet cheerful Rolles at **Rolle Town,** east of George Town, where there are ave-era ruins and an unusual, ell-maintained marble tomb f a young loyalist mother and er infant who died in 1792.

Pretty Molly Bay deserves its djective. It's named after a nermaid who sits on a rock in he moonlight, said to be seen nore clearly after a few drinks. Coco plums and sea grapes ringe the beach and the leserted offshore **Pigeon Cay** vhere there's even better sand.

The Tropic of Cancer crosses he island in the area where a ridge (called The Ferry) conects Great Exuma to Little Exuma.

Sparsely inhabited today, **Little Exuma** knew prosperity when cotton was king in the 18th century. You'll see considerable remains of a plantation manor and slave huts at WILLIAMS TOWN. Nearby, a tall off-white column which used to signal the location of salt beds to passing ships, is still standing. Today only a few islanders take salt from the flats glistening in the sun.

Stretching protectively offshore between the Atlantic breakers and the George Town area is slim **Stocking Island,** coconut and palmetto palms waving along a ridge behind inviting beaches. Shelling can be worthwhile on this island which, while only minutes away by boat from the resort area opposite, feels like a remote desert island. There's also an interesting sea cave for divers.

Traveling by rented car or motorbike, you'll find the potholed road heading north from George Town a somewhat hazardous drive. But it's hard to fault the scenery along the 3-mile **Silver Beach** with its casuarina trees and azure water swooshing over coral reefs.

The 700 residents of **Rolleville,** a palm-tree-and-woodenhouses settlement in the far north, include more Rolles **65** than all the other family names taken together. Shy at first because they don't see many strangers, villagers quickly warm to your interest. They'll point out their four churches, the primary school and hilltop drinking establishment, show off their babies, and tell you about the Sunday evening dance with live music. At SAND DOLLAR beach and elsewhere nearby, there is good shelling. You might hear about the mysterious Jack M'Lantern who still roams the Exuma cays in a phantom vessel, scaring boatmen as he has for centuries.

Twelve miles north of Rolleville along the string of cays, at LEE STOCKING ISLAND, you might arrange a visit to a marine research station studying the little-known life stages of the crawfish. Farther up the chain, several deserted cays constitute a migratory bird preserve.

From **Staniel Cay,** an important yacht haven and trim little settlement, visitors are taken to "Thunderball Grotto" where still more of that James Bond adventure was filmed. At the smaller boating center of SAMPSON CAY, those in search of tranquillity may like to take a Boston whaler or similar small craft and explore the cays of nearby **Pipe Creek.**

The prized **Exuma Cay Land and Sea Park** extend north for 22 miles from CONCH CUT to WAX CAY CUT. Gorgeous coral reefs, crowded with fish, nature trails, wild beaches with dunes, several dozen species of birds in tropical vegetation or ocean cliffs are all part of this 177-square-mile preserve founded by the Bahamas National Trust. Boating, wandering and viewing while snorkeling are activities which are positively encouraged. Bear in mind, however, that no flora or fauna may be removed.

Andros

Largest and least known of the major populated islands of the Bahamas, Andros is fascinating. From the air and the sea the great **coral reef** running the length of the island is tremendously impressive. This scuba and snorkel wonderland is not a barrier reef, experts say, but the world's second largest fringing reef, surpassed only in the Red Sea. It marks the dizzying drop-off into the blueblack depths of the Tongue of the Ocean where huge fish and submarines cruise.

Dotting Andros' 2,300 square miles (three times the size of any other Bahamian island), or just offshore, are more than 100 ocean holes

better known as blue holes although inland they're often green or brownish. Sea water forced in through countless underground fissures causes their water levels to rise or fall with the tides. Creeks running through Andros divide it into segments, some large enough to have individual names.

Unusual undersea thrills attract scuba divers to the Andros reef.

Much of the interior is untracked bush or pine forest. Several species of orchids thrive here. Iguanas four feet long are still found, as are **67**

small diamond-patterned boa constrictors (snakes abound in the Bahamas, particularly constrictors called "chicken snakes" or "fowl snakes," but there are no poisonous species), magnificent butterflies, and ospreys and herons. The only menace when exploring the bush is poison wood, a mottled tree which if touched can give you a serious rash.

Marine biologists report that there are some 32,000 species of marine life offshore from Andros, particularly on the reef. All the major game fish, nine species of sharks, giant turtles and stands of many types of coral help enliven the Tongue of the Ocean. The shallows afford great bone-fishing.

The 10,000 natives of Andros live in settlements along the east coast sheltered by the reef, and in the north. Also scattered widely here are about a dozen tourist facilities reached by five airports: South Andros (Congo Town), Mangrove Cay, Andros Town, San Andros and Andros Central. There's no civilization on the island's muddy and marshy western side.

South Andros boasts the lovely coconut palm beach of **Long Bay Cay** and various attractive, little-visited creeks where fishing, crabbing and bird watching are excellent.

Heading north, the next major segment of Andros is **Mangrove Cay,** beyond the large cross-island water course called South Bight. In the shallows where Lisbon Creek runs into South Bight, there's an area of undersea caverns and coral teeming with fish which provides as exciting snorkeling as you'll find anywhere in the Bahamas (see p. 113). Cousteau and other undersea spe-

Above: Small Hope Bay's beach bistro leaves nothing to be desired.
Left: Andros inhabitant models clothes worthy of a Parisian couturier.

cialists have explored the spectacular **Linda Cay Blue Hole
cave** here. Even if you don't
snorkel, take a boat around this
amazing area. There are some
tourist accommodations at the
friendly little palm tree and
boat building settlement of **Lisbon Creek,** named in 1818 after George Lisbon, a slave
trader who prospered with banana and hardwood timber
plantations. Mangrove Cay has
movies just twice a month and
many families keep goats and
sheep. Why do people like living here? "We don't have to go
buy a coconut like in Nassau.
We just go under the tree and
wait for it to ripen and fall off." **69**

Evil Elves?

You'd have to be terribly unlucky to be bothered by the legendarily mischievous Andros creature, the chickcharney. Dismissed as a myth by much of the modern generation, but still a useful device to frighten children into good behavior, the red-eyed, three-toed chickcharnies are said to hang from pine trees and to cause all kinds of misfortune including illness and shortening of life. One expert thinks the belief began with a real but now extinct barn owl.

You may well meet Androsians who soberly insist they have seen chickcharnies. One recent sighting was of a "featherless, chickenlike creature which hissed like a cat." If you do spot one, be warned not to laugh or turn your back: your head might instantly be wrenched around 180 degrees.

Around the FRESH CREEK/SMALL HOPE BAY area further north the scene is somewhat livelier. At **Andros Town** a thriving little batik factory shows you how to design your own piece of material. In Fresh Creek, New Yorkers may enjoy trying to ferret out the full story behind a wrecked Staten Island ferry boat.

No outsider will have much luck penetrating the military security at the Atlantic Undersea Test and Evaluation Center (AUTEC) headquarters here. It's known that U.S. and allied naval warfare systems are tested at depths of more than a mile in the Tongue of the Ocean, and it's not unusual to see American nuclear submarines on the surface. Half a dozen AUTEC stations along Andros electronically track every movement of the occasional Cuban "trawler" or Soviet submarine which ventures into this great underwater chasm.

For snorkelers or novice divers, a cut through the reef called **Love Hill Channel** offers beautiful stands of coral and many fish on a white sand bottom. For shell, driftwood and bottle collectors there are miles of deserted beaches. Swimmers will like the coconut tree beach at the pleasant little settlement of STANIARD CREEK.

In the far north there are good beaches at EVANS BAY around **Morgan's Cave,** a 300-foot-deep grotto, named after the pirate Morgan, which you can explore with a flashlight. NICOLL'S TOWN is a peaceful settlement spread among palm trees. It and SAN ANDROS have tourist facilities. Friendly natives may tell you about churches popular because they have "sweet music"—hymns with guitars.

Near their airport, North Androsians proudly point out two reservoirs which hold "the water for Nassau." The capital depends largely on fresh water barged in from here.

Berry Islands

There are more millionaires per square mile in this string of delightful cays than in most places on earth, but ordinary travelers are also welcome. In fact, the 30 islets in the Berries only amount to a total of about a dozen square miles, and people of any kind are scarce. Just two have resort facilities and commercial air service: semi-private Chub Cay at the chain's southern tip, and Great Harbour Cay in the north. Aside from a smattering of private cays, the rest are deserted.

Sport fishing is overwhelmingly the name of the game at **Chub Cay** where some yacht owners at the marina use smaller yachts as runabouts. Anglers emphatically report that here at the top of the Tongue of the Ocean, billfish such as marlin run in greater numbers, if not in size, than at rival Bimini. There's also good bonefishing in the flats up through the Berries.

Scuba divers and snorkelers are just beginning to discover the underwater marvels hereabouts. The shallow coral reef off **Mamma Rhoda Rock,** a brief motorboat ride from Chub Cay marina, is an outstanding experience. Through shallows elsewhere run "rivers," deeper channels where many crawfish lurk under rocks, usually sharing holes with moray eels. For beach lovers, there are 3 miles of good sand backed by casuarinas at **Queen's Beach.** And for shelling, a sandy shoal called **Sand Dollar Hill** is about $2^1/_2$ miles out from the marina.

Atop a hill on **Hoffman Cay** up the chain, is a blue hole more than 600 feet deep which attracts scuba divers off Miami cruise boats. The only living things found thus far in the hole have been oysters.

Great Harbour Cay, originally projected to be an international jet set preserve some years ago, has especially pretty hills. Low silver-top palms and sea grape are all over this breezy island, and you'll find marvelous beaches. At the impressive marina, yachtsmen park in slips beneath their townhouses, walking up to their living rooms from their marine garages.

The island's population is slightly more than 500, mostly natives living in the casual settlement of **Bullocks Harbour** across a channel on BAMBOO CAY. To get there you must traverse a 200-yard-long bridge unlike anything in the Bahamas: whenever a small boat toots three times for passage, a genial keeper cranks the bridge open by hand while cars and pedestrians wait. In Bullocks Harbour you'll see the police station drowsing under palm trees, the island's one public telephone, two churches and the mail boat pier which explodes with activity once a week.

Perhaps the most attractive place in the Bahamas is about 5 miles from the airport in the barely inhabited north of the island. Called **Sugar Beach Caves,** this is an area of small sandy coves set among cliffs, reminiscent of the best Mediterranean beaches. Swimming here is inviting, but there's an undertow at times.

Farther south on the same coast you'll find a fine strip of open beach, with good snorkeling opposite HAINES CAY. In the same area, at SHARK ROCK the shelling can be excellent at low tide.

Bimini

Hemingway loved it. So did New York politician Adam Clayton Powell. That was years ago. Today Bimini's far-flung fame rests not on celebrities but on the sea around it. Or rather, the Gulf Stream which flows just offshore, the haunt of the many very big ones that don't get away.

The "fishing capital of the world" the locals call it, dismissing counter-claims from Florida or the Caribbean. Along the **Alice Town** marina-hotel-restaurant strip you'll see pictures proudly posted of world record deep sea catches by boats out of Bimini. In highest season when tournaments are underway, more than 100 fishing boats dock here, with every angler aware of the saying, "You can catch a big game fish five minutes out of Bimini harbour." And you learn that if you do land a big one, it could cost you $1,000 to have it mounted for display.

The nautical excitement is on **North Bimini,** a flat and sandy 7-mile strip separated from sleepier South Bimini by a narrow channel. You'll find various reminders of Hemingway, who was inspired by the island to write *The Old Man and the Sea.* Earlier he had written much of *To Have and*

Family Islands have lots of room for those beautiful Bahamian children (one Andros family has 18); the baby boom in Bimini is pretty good, too.

Have Not while staying at an anglers' hotel here which displays photographs of the young Hemingway machine-gunning sharks and showing off the different game fish he'd caught.

There's a decisively American atmosphere in Bimini, which is just 50 miles due east of Miami—a 30-minute seaplane flight or a bracing boat run across the Gulf Stream. There's also a prodigious amount of drinking along the marina row. Liquor store dealers, today's counterparts of the warehousemen who used to work here during Prohibition, say some boats "use more liquor than fuel."

Strolling north away from Alice Town's bustle, you'll see the more typically Family Island settlements of BAILEY TOWN, PORGY BAY and PARADISE POINT where most of Bimini's 1,600 residents have their wooden homes. If you'd like to trudge out into the bush and

mangrove swamps, someone will direct you to two alleged sites of the Fountain of Youth which Ponce de León, Spanish governor of Puerto Rico, unsuccessfully sought in 1513. (He discovered Florida instead.) One site is on North Bimini and the other on South Bimini.

Another controversial Bimini sight lies in 15 feet of water offshore. These are huge stone blocks symmetrically arranged on the bottom which resemble walls or roadways. Snorkeling or diving to explore them, you can make your own mind up about assertions that these are evidence of a "megalithic Atlantis" of 8,000 or more years ago. Most experts reject this notion.

Around Bimini are interesting undersea opportunities including outstanding diving along the offshore ocean wall. The island also has stretches of reasonable beach, often with palm trees.

Note: For details on fish and game fishing see pages 91 and 92.

Modest house with Hemingway family connections. The author also lived in Key West and Havana.

Excursions

Florida

Only 45 minutes by jet from Nassau lies one of the most popular states in America—Florida*. There are a number of one-day tours from Nassau and Freeport to Miami as well as other longer trips including a shoppers package and a tour to Orlando with Disney World admission. You can also take a regular fare and make up your own itinerary according to your special interests.

With an area of over 58,000 square miles, the longest coastline of any state in America excluding Alaska and a mild, sunny climate, Florida has always been a center for vacations. But for visitors day-tripping from the Bahamas, beaches will take second place to Florida's unique attractions.

Miami

This surprising metropolis is America's youngest big city; development only began in 1896 when the Florida East Coast railroad was extended to the region. Today, cruise-ships, yachts, fishing boats and freighters keep the waterfront humming while traffic never ceases along the futuristic net-work of swooping expressways. At night Miami's skyscraper-studded skyline glitters, lighting up for the area's 1½ million residents.

The city's blend of accents is intriguing. You'll hear all manner of American accents: Eastern, Southern, Mid-Western—and most noticeably, Latin. More than one-third of the inhabitants are Hispanic, most of them refugee Cubans, many of whom live in **Little Havana.** It's worth exploring this mushrooming city-within-a-city full of small shops, cafés and restaurants with sidewalk terraces.

Guided coach tours take you the length of heavily built-up **Miami Beach,** past nearly 400 hotels of every size and category, and through a fancy residential district nicknamed "Condominium Canyon". You'll see where American political conventions have been held, hear about celebrities who flocked to this palm-tree strip during its boom periods, about the beach-front hotel with more than $1 million worth of chandeliers, about people who can afford new homes today in areas where land costs thousands of dollars

---

* For a more complete tour of the state, see the Berlitz travel guide FLORIDA.

a square foot. Money mania? Definitely.

In North Miami, tour buses stop at the **Spanish Monastery** with a lovely cloister. Built in 1141 in Segovia province of Spain, it was transported stone by stone to the U.S. in 1925 by American newspaper magnate William Randolph Hearst. The flags hanging in the chapel were obtained from a Madrid museum and date from the 12th to 15th centuries.

In a suburban area visitors may be taken to a private home where large fish swim in an aquarium built into the front wall, visible from the street. At **Hialeah Racetrack,**

On Biscayne Bay, high-rise glamor of booming subtropical vacationland.

non-gamblers will enjoy the flamingoes. Bettors can also "go to the dogs"—very popular greyhound races.

In **Coral Gables,** discreet retreat of the rich and very rich, look for beautiful Columbus Boulevard, arched over by spectacular banyan trees. In this area some residents park their yachts in waterways beneath their back porches.

South of metropolitan Miami, you'll see hundreds of colorful parrots, macaws, flamingoes and other tropical

birds in the rain forest foliage of the **Parrot Jungle.** Particularly noted for its orchids (and good for picnics), the **Fairchild Tropical Garden** has even more exotic greenery. **Metrozoo,** a cageless facility, displays animals compatible with the south Florida climate.

At fashionably "bohemian" **Coconut Grove** you'll see droves of joggers and other athletes exercising under the palm trees. Bahamian timber schooner laborers are given credit for settling Coconut Grove where today, it's said, the price of the most expensive condominium runs into hundreds of thousands of dollars.

Vizcaya, an Italianate mansion set in 10 acres of formal gardens, is now a museum with 70 rooms full of treasures. One of the first Miami millionaires, James Deering, hired a huge team of workmen to construct the house about 60 years ago. See the breakwater offshore, in the form of Cleopatra's barge.

Take the Rickenbacker Causeway from Miami to Key Biscayne to get to one of Miami's star attractions, the marvellous 60-acre **Seaquarium.** This is the sort of place where you can spend a whole day without losing interest. You'll see dozens of exotic creatures from the ocean depths. Watch them being fed in the gigantic aquarium tanks, then join up with the crowd outside to see one of the shows. The most spectacular of them features a 9,500 pound killer whale who leaps gracefully more than 20 feet out of the water, only to fall back again in a thunderous crescendo of dazzling spray.

Flipper, seen on TV in some 30 countries, climaxes his show with an amazing double-flip leap out of the water. He and dolphin companions play basketball, carry trainers on their backs, do tail dances and belly-roll high dives, and perform a "water ballet" with their trainers in the pool. (Dolphins are so much a part of the local scene that the name of the hugely popular professional football team is the Miami Dolphins. As many as 84,000 fans may jam the Orange Bowl stadium to watch a game.)

The Seaquarium, billed as south Florida's leading tourist attraction, also has a shark channel where many rather small sharks (perhaps 5 feet) go into a frenzy at feeding time. In placid contrast nearby, the park exhibits the first baby manatee (sea cow) conceived and born in an artificial environment.

The Everglades

About 40 miles southwest of metropolitan Miami are the vast mangrove swamps of Everglades National Park, home for a host of slithering creatures. Whether you visit in your own car or on an excursion, you'll see how Florida looked before the onslaught of bulldozers, cranes and drainage canals. Extending over 2,000 square miles, the area teems with everything from alligators and tree snails to butterflies and birds.

The huge swamp is filled with small islands called hammocks and is planned to allow visitors easy access to all the top sights. Thousands of different kinds of tropical plants, birds and animals abound and you can see them from a space-age airboat (a hovercraft designed to skim over the swampy saw grass on a cushion of air). Other means of transportation for happy viewing include a tram (with a commentary given by a guide) and sign-posted nature trails, or you can even hire a houseboat to glide you through the mangroves.

There are two entrances to the Everglades, one off Tamiami Trail and the other south of Homestead. The park is open all year round.

Key West

Only 160 miles southwest of Miami the mighty peninsula of Florida tapers off in a graceful arc of 1,000 islands extending for nearly 100 miles into the Gulf of Mexico. These islands, the Florida Keys, are joined by what must be one of the world's longest—and most spectacular—overwater roads, the **Overseas Highway** as it's known. One of the bridges is 7 miles long.

Key West itself remains a historic town full of nostalgia. It was here that the summer White House stood during the Truman administration. John James Audubon, the famous naturalist and artist, lived and worked here 150 years ago. The charming white **Audubon house** is full of beautiful furniture and memorabilia. Writers have looked to America's southernmost city ever since Ernest Hemingway set up house in the town in a building reminiscent of an era that can usually only be seen in TV re-runs. You can still visit Hemingway's favorite Key West bar, Sloppy Joe's, where he used to spend much of his time working. This local institution is air-cooled by old-fashioned paddle fans. Be sure to go for a ride on the "Conch Train", a tourist tram with commentary that goes past all the sights of town.

If all else fails in Key West (and you're feeling homesick for Nassau skin-diving) you can always take the plunge. Head back via **Key Largo** just off the Florida coast—you'll find most of the familiar fish as well as glass-bottom boats in the John Pennekamp Coral Reef Underwater Park.

Walt Disney World

They call it the "happiest place on earth," which may be why more visitors now come here than to any other single attraction anywhere. Surprisingly, four of every five are adults.

Dedicated to "…the philosophy and life of Walt Elias Disney" and spread over 27,400 land and waterscaped acres of central Florida, Disney World is styled as the most complete vacation destination in existence, with sightseeing, sports, nightlife, shopping, camping, hotels and restaurants. The accent throughout is on wholesome, family-oriented entertainment.

Heart of things is the 100-acre Magic Kingdom, where it's easy to confuse who's real

More American than apple pie: Cinderella Castle at Disney World.

Mini-cars are among most popular of the do-it-yourself attractions.

and who's artificial. Just to the south of it is what might be called its brain, EPCOT Center, a multi-media projection of the world's past and future filtered through a Disney-inspired imagination.

The **Magic Kingdom** area has six sections: "Main Street, U.S.A." with a re-creation of turn-of-the-century America facing the much photographed Cinderella Castle; "Adventureland" with unusual rides; "Frontierland" with America's old west; "Liberty Square" with patriotic American displays; "Fantasyland" with entertainment inspired by Walt Disney films; and "Tomorrowland" with futuristic displays.

Among the 45 shows and "adventures", don't miss "It's a Small World", an enchanting sail past hundreds of moving dolls from many countries; and the "Haunted Mansion" where you journey through a wackily eerie house while bones rattle, ghouls groan and grave stones shake. "Pirates of the Caribbean" is another funny boat ride where the swashbucklers are so cleverly crafted that you duck their swinging cutlasses.

For a gentle overview of the entire Magic Kingdom, try the aerial tramway in the evening as the lights are coming on. During the summer and the two weeks around Easter, the "Main Street Electrical Parade" is staged, which is a dazzling spectacle of floats with half a million colored lights.

Out of Walt Disney's last dream of an Experimental Prototype Community of Tomorrow has grown his company's most ambitious project, the **EPCOT Center**—partly built, constantly evolving—south of the Magic Kingdom. It attempts nothing less than to present in exciting visual terms the past and future of our planet together with a showcase of some of the world's nations, all within a few hundred acres around an artificial lake.

Disney World is about 20 miles southwest of Orlando off Interstate Highway 4. It is open daily far into the night at peak periods. If you have the choice, mid-October to mid-December is the best time to visit. One-day excursions by *bus* from Miami are not recommended.

Sea World of Florida

A 7,000-pound killer whale is the astonishing attraction at this exciting marine park. The genial black and white monster, named Shamu, leaps entirely out of the water, stands on his head waving his enormous tail, lets handlers ride him around the tank, nods his head to questions and has kissed some 4,000 incredulous tourists. Shamu is nearly 22 feet long and perhaps 15 years old. He eats 200 pounds of food a day and more than 50 vitamin pills. As rewards for responding to slight signals from his trainers, he likes to have his tongue rubbed and his back scratched.

Around Sea World's 135 acres, look also for the splendid dolphin ballet, a trainer riding on two dolphins' backs, sea lions playing volleyball, and a seal and otter show. Children can feed various creatures.

Sea World, 12 miles southwest of Orlando at I-4 and the Bee Line Expressway, is only a few minutes drive from Disney World. It's open daily, with one admission charge covering all shows.

Cypress Gardens

Cypress Gardens, about 50 miles south of Orlando, is a sea of tropical vegetation basking in a luxuriant landscaped setting worthy of any Hollywood movie set. So, it won't be surprising to learn that many TV shows and commercials are shot here. But Cypress Gardens' unique attraction is the incredible water-ski show performed up to four times daily.

Spectators, whether skiers themselves or not, will be astounded—and delighted—at the acrobatics performed by the experts. It may look easy but it took months, even years, of rigorous discipline to master the art of these graceful water dances.

Standing on each others' shoulders, whizzing over

A LEM (Lunar Excursion Module in NASA terminology) reposes on the grass. Already a museum piece.

ramps, forming geometric patterns with amazing precision, the performers are towed around the lake in a ballet vaguely reminiscent of Busby Berkeley movies and the old Radio City chorus line.

Programs vary, but you may be lucky enough to see one number which ends spectacularly as some of the skiers suddenly release the rope and glide effortlessly into the area in front of the audience right up onto the beach.

Kennedy Space Center

Only 45 miles east of Orlando, on Cape Canaveral, stands one of the most advanced complexes of technological gadgetry anywhere—the John F. Kennedy Space Center. Spread over 220 square miles, the vast base is an engineer's dream-come-true. As you admire lunar modules, Saturn V/Apollo rockets, space shuttle and skylab hardware, you'll find it difficult to believe that only 67 years before men landed on the moon in 1969, no engine-powered machine had ever been in the air.

You'll be taken round on a guided bus tour* and you may even be lucky enough to visit on a launch day (earth satellites, space probes and other research equipment are routinely launched from the Cape). But even if you don't get to see a launch, you can still visit the mammoth vehicle assembly building (so high and spacious that it is said clouds sometimes form inside) as well as seeing many other aspects of space technology in the National Aeronautics and Space Administration Museum.

For all its electronic marvels, the Kennedy Space Center has not forgotten those tiny self-powered miracles—the birds. The U.S. Department of the Interior looks after some 140,000 acres of land and water in a reservation within the spaceport. As well as birds, many reptiles, amphibians and other animals find refuge here. Some of these areas can be visited: take Routes 402 or 406 from Titusville.

The Dark Continent/Busch Gardens

One of western Florida's most popular tourist attractions, this 300-acre theme park features more than 800 animals and 2,500 birds. They're all real, if you're confused after Disney World.

---

* The route varies for operational reasons.

Touring on foot or by monorail, riverboat or llama-drawn wagon, you'll see a dozen rare Bengal tigers dunking themselves in waterfalls, baby chimpanzees having their diapers changed, ring-tailed lemurs lazing and golden-rumped agouti grazing. Children will enjoy swinging on Tarzan vines, riding elephants and petting bushbucks and other animals their own size, or enormous Galapagos tortoises. There are over 60 different species of creatures including exotic macaws, parrots and flamingoes. Inside a "nocturnal mountain" in perpetual gloom, you can observe boa constrictors, huge Burmese pythons and other reptiles.

More commercially, at a "Moroccan" bazaar snake charmers, belly dancers and jugglers with southern American accents perform. For those with iron nerves, the park has frightening rides, including the Python, described as "Florida's ultimate thrill ride."

Often called just Busch Gardens, the park is an hour's drive west of Disney World, 8 miles northeast of downtown Tampa (2 miles east on Interstate 75 and the Busch Boulevard interchange). It's open daily with one admission fee covering all shows, rides and

86 sightseeing.

What to Do

Sports

Whichever of the warm-weather sports you prefer, facilities abound around these islands and the Bahamian climate lets you indulge 12 months a year. Sunshine is also the only potential bad news: the semitropical rays are wicked on newly arrived skins, so that if you don't curtail your exposure for the first several days, painful sunburn will do it for you—regardless of how much suntan oil you use. Unexpectedly, this is just as true even when you're under water.

Swimming

Every island you'll visit has wonderful swimming from good beaches—some 630 miles of them. When you first splash into the gorgeous aquamarine water over a white sand bottom, you'll start to appreciate the true magic of the Bahamas

Surf may be higher on eastern shores, often exposed to the open Atlantic. Islanders can advise if there's an undertow which might be dangerous for children or weak swimmers

Otherwise, commonsense precautions are obvious (only at large resort areas might you find lifeguards). Do *not* swim between dusk and dawn.

The very best beaches in the Bahamas include: Sugar Beach Caves on Great Harbour Cay; Fernandez Bay on Cat Island; Pink Sands Beach on Harbour Island; Paradise Beach on Paradise Island; Calabash Bay on Long Island; French Leave on Eleuthera; Old Fort Beach and parts of Cable Beach on New Providence; Treasure Cay, Abaco.

For those allergic to sand, most hotels have swimming pools.

Snorkeling and Scuba Diving

Undersea viewing is the incomparably beautiful experience in the Bahamas, memorable for the novice snorkeler or the world-traveled diver alike. Visibility is remarkable in these warm waters amid islands with no sediment-carrying rivers. So too, almost everywhere, is the array of marine life. Even some coral reefs immediately offshore from hotel beaches are full of brilliantly colored fish.

Snorkel masks and fins are rented cheaply or sold on all tourist islands. If you can float and breathe through your mouth, you can pick up snorkeling within minutes. People you'll see snorkeling in T-shirts are smart enough to respect the searing sun.

Just possibly, the best of the hundreds of great shallow snorkeling sites may be: off **Lisbon Creek** on Andros, and at the **Fowl Cay** and **Pelican Cay** underwater parks in the Abacos.

The Bahamas have more scuba resorts than any country down in the Caribbean: diving facilities are now available at some 25 sites on 18 islands, including a few of the world's best. You'll find these types of dives: reef, wall, cave, drift, ocean-blue hole and wreck. Underwater photography is taught at only some of the dive sites. (Buy your underwater film at home—it will be less expensive and more reliable.) Short resort courses in scuba (the acronym for self-contained underwater breathing apparatus) will teach you basic safety techniques and practical aspects of the sport, enabling you to undertake shallow dives very quickly. Certain dive sites provide more advanced instruction.

Fishing with spear guns or any triggered device is illegal everywhere in the Bahamas. In **87**

some areas spear-fishing is permitted with a Hawaiian sling or pole spear, but only when free diving, never with scuba gear. No fishing or collecting of any kind is allowed in areas designated as national parks or within one mile of the entire northern shore of New Providence, which includes Paradise Island.

When you see the sad damage caused by people in some areas, you'll appreciate that no part of a coral reef should ever be removed. Unless you're positive about identifying marine life, it's best to touch nothing.

Fire coral causes a nasty burn, lettuce and other corals can cut. Also avoid sea urchins which are round and black (less often white) with porcupine spines; bristle worms which look like centipedes and cause a severe burn; occasional jellyfish (Portuguese men-of-war); and stinging hydroids which are white, feathery organisms resembling snowflakes.

The greatest underwater menace is not sharks or any other creature, but the sun, as far down as 30 feet. The rays are particularly dangerous because, aside from striking you directly, they're also reflected off light sandy bottoms and back off the surface.

Few people have been fortunate enough to dive throughout the Bahamas. One expert who has believes the two finest sites are off the southwestern corner of San Salvador and between Highbourn and Staniel Cays in the Exumas, which includes the Land and Sea Park.

For an island-by-island summary of diving highspots see page 113 in the blueprint section of this book.

Boating

Yachtsmen argue about which of the two superb cruising areas of the Bahamas is better—Abaco's great arch of an inland sea or Exuma's long chain of cays. The Berry Island archipelago is smaller but also popular. Most boaters arrive from Florida and pass through such major marina centers as Bimini, Nassau-Paradise, West End and Freeport/Lucaya. At certain places you can fly in and charter sailboats or power cruisers of various sizes, some

crewed, some bareboat. Note that fresh water may be in short supply at various Family Island docks.

Regattas are a consuming passion of the Bahamians, particularly those featuring native-built boats such as the annual affairs at George Town, Exuma, Salt Pond, Long Island, and Mangrove Cay, Andros. The Miami–Nassau race of ocean-going yachts followed by the Nassau Cup race attracts international attention. **89**

Other Watersports

Major hotel watersports centers or independent operators nearby offer water-skiing, windsurfing and small sailboat rental at hourly rates or, occasionally, as part of prepaid vacation packages.

Para-sailing, soaring overhead in a parachute harness pulled by a speedboat, is increasingly popular at Cable Beach, Paradise Island and Lucaya. Landings on a raft seem effortless.

Twin Silos Beach on the windward side of Eleuthera south of Gregory Town, known locally as Surfers' Beach, is the only serious surfing site in the Bahamas.

Fishing

As every deep-sea angler has heard, Bahamas waters offer some of the world's greatest game fishing. Currently the Bahamas holds about two dozen world records for game fish, including blue and white marlin, wahoo, bluefin, skipjack tuna, and dolphin; some were caught by amateurs wise enough to listen to their Bahamian guides and skippers. At almost every tourist island in the Commonwealth you can charter fishing boats by the half-day, full day or week. Seasonal tournaments are staged at major fishing centers.

Many experts now agree that in general Exuma Sound, particularly south of Cat Island, is the finest sport fishing area in the Bahamas, superior to such other outstanding haunts as Bimini, Cat Cay, Walker's Cay, West End, Chub Cay and Abaco.

Blue marlin, king of the Atlantic game fish, run throughout open Bahamian waters, in greatest numbers in the summer. They may be bigger in the Gulf Stream, but Chub Cay anglers insist there are more blues off the Berries.

White marlin, smaller cousins of the blues, are found in deep water from winter and spring. Best fishing seems to be off Bimini.

Sailfish, with the dramatic dorsal fins and long bills, run best from spring through summer.

Wahoo, perhaps the fastest fish in the ocean, are most plentiful from winter into spring. Gigantic wahoo have been reported in Bahamian waters.

Bluefin tuna, which grow to huge sizes, migrate in great schools through the Bahamas only between mid-April and mid-June.

Blackfin and **skipjack** 91

(oceanic bonito) tuna appear in schools during the summer.

Yellowfin or Allison tuna, less frequent, are usually caught in the summer.

Dolphin, colorful, fine eating fish (not related to the gray air-breathing mammals also called porpoises) are found in deep water primarily in winter and spring.

Barracuda, found year-round, are brought in by sport anglers in greater numbers than any other fish.

Grouper, much the most popular eating fish in the country, are found in reef areas everywhere.

Bonefish. The challenging shallow-water and light-tackle sport of bonefishing, beloved by many anglers above all else, is perhaps best in the Joulter Cays flats off north Andros. Other prime bonefish locations: Great Exuma, Bimini, Walker's Cay, Glenton's Sound, Millerton and Deadman's Cay on Long Island, the Berry Islands, and parts of Abaco and Eleuthera.

Golf

Around the Bahamas there are a number of championship courses, with predictable arguments about which is the best.

Many top U.S. professionals have played Bahamian courses. Rental clubs, golf carts and lessons are normally available. Some resorts offer golf packages.

Grand Bahama is the most golf-oriented island. The top course is Lucayan Golf & Country Club with 18 holes. Other 18-hole courses on the island are at the Bahamas Princess Hotel and Fortune Hills Club, the only rolling course.

New Providence boasts one of the best, at the Divi Bahamas Beach Resort and Country Club, designed by Joe Lee, par 72, course record 66. Also on New Providence are the Ambassador Beach Hotel course and the Lyford Cay Club, and across the channel is the Paradise Island course (18 holes).

On Eleuthera, Cotton Bay is the course Robert Trent Jones reportedly considers the finest he's ever designed.

Treasure Cay Club on Abaco, par 72.

Horseback Riding

Horse riding is available on New Providence and Grand Bahama. Stables on both islands provide guided tours but they don't take young children.

Private Flying

A large and growing number of private pilots come to the Bahamas each year. Around the islands there are about 50 airfields ranging from sophisticated Nassau and Freeport to very rudimentary short strips. An annual Bahamas Flying Treasure Hunt is staged in which small-plane pilots swoop low over the islands looking for clues to the "treasure."

The Bahamas Ministry of Tourism produces a useful flight planning chart covering the islands.

Tennis and Squash

The Bahamas has about 150 courts, with more abuilding. While most are on New Providence-Paradise and Grand Bahama, you'll find some tennis on all tourist Family Islands and major operations at such sites as Treasure Cay, Abaco, Windmere Island and Cotton Bay, Eleuthera. Tournaments are held on Paradise Island and at Cable Beach.

Many hotels have instructors, ball machines and all-weather courts illuminated for night play. There are clay, plexipave and acrylic surfaces.

Visiting squash addicts will be welcome at courts in Nassau and Freeport.

Shopping

Though not duty-free, the Bahamas offers a range of European and Commonwealth goods at prices far lower than in the United States. Local craftsmen who have resisted mass-production to satisfy surging tourist demand produce some distinctive souvenirs.

Bay Street in Nassau and the International Bazaar in Freeport are the major tourist shopping areas, but Family Islanders often sell hand-crafted items, and some resorts have boutiques.

Stores are generally open from about 9 a.m. to 5 p.m., closed Sundays, holidays and possibly Thursday, Friday or Saturday afternoon. The Nassau and Freeport straw markets are open every day and even after dark you'll probably be able to find someone selling straw items. Many shops will mail your purchases abroad.

Bargaining at outdoor stalls,

something of a standard tourist pastime with the straw ladies, might get you a discount. But don't bother trying in regular stores where you pay the posted price. There is no sales tax in the Bahamas.

Best Buys

Among authentic local items, look for:

Coconut-shell jewelry and **artifacts.** These are said to be so nearly indestructible that they will "outlast the wearer." On

Harbour Island off Eleuthera, if probably not elsewhere, look for lamps crafted from coconut husks.

Paintings. Several Bahamian artists do interesting work based on local themes.

Printed fabrics, particularly Androsian hand-waxed and dyed fabrics with island designs from a Fresh Creek, Andros, batik factory are on sale in Nassau, Freeport and at major Family Island resorts.

Rum. Eleuthera pineapple rum tops Bahamian liquid products. You'll also see regular and coconut rum.

Shells and other items from the sea. Conch shells, if you didn't get one off the bottom yourself, are common and you should bargain before you buy. Polished clam shells and seashell ashtrays are further possibilities, as are sponges. Jewelry from the sea includes articles fashioned from conch shell, whelk shell and black coral as well as sharks' teeth, sand dollars, fish-scale combs, etc.

Straw goods. In the tremendous array of mostly routine straw work, try to find the now-rare straw airplanes complete

Americans and Canadians may now take home several hundreds of dollars worth of duty-free purchases. **95**

with pilot, or detailed straw models of Nassau surreys.

Wood-carvings. A small fraction of the wood-carving you'll see is of good quality, but model boats from gum-elemi wood are often quite intricate and worth considering.

Imported Goods

With tariffs recently cut on various imports, you should find particularly interesting bargains in: china, crystal, French perfumes, Scottish and English woolens (cashmere may be 40 per cent cheaper than in the U.S., and even slightly lower than U.K. prices), linen, leather, Japanese cameras (savings as much as 50 per cent over U.S. prices are advertised), watches, liquor, tobacco products including Cuban cigars, and luxury non-American cigarette lighters. Knowledgeable shoppers will want to consider Mexican silver jewelry and South American emeralds.

Recently many visitors have been buying gold—chains, pendants, bars, coins. Bars of silver and even platinum are also on sale.

Nassau and Freeport offer a range of sophisticated shops, while top Family Island hotels have boutiques.

Nightlife

...round the Bahamas much of
...e after-dark action is concen-
...ated in resort hotels. You'll
...nd cocktail lounges, discos
...nd a smattering of native
...ws at larger resort complex-
..., more basic drink-and-dance
...ubs and a very few cabaret-
...pe spots in non-tourist areas.
...our hotel's employees may
...ell stage an imaginative
...ahamian revue of their own
...evising, with skits, beat music,
...mbo contests and boisterous
...arades all competing for at-
...ntion.

Wherever you are out for the
...vening be prepared for local
...nthusiasts to sashay up and
...ax you into dancing. That's
...art of the fun in these islands
...ll so dedicated to relaxation
...nd having a good time. Some
...f the Bahamian songs you'll
...ear are decidedly risqué, with
...eanings clear even if certain
...ucial words are bleeped out
...y the vocalists. Apart from
...urrent American pop tunes,
...ere's a variety of other mu-
...c including goombay, reg-
...ae and calypso.

Some of the cinemas in Nas-
...u and Freeport occasionally
...ow good quality first-run
...ovies, but the usual fare is
...ging westerns, horror, occult
...d disaster films.

Gambling

Shades of Las Vegas, you may
think when you see the suave
gentlemen with sunglasses
patrolling the darkened casinos
on Paradise Island, Cable
Beach and in Freeport. You
are exceedingly welcome to put
your money in perpetually

Junkanoo

There's nothing like a festival,
and the colorful, traditional
Goombay Summer Carnival
was calculated to keep the fun
going all through the off-
season. Folklore events, art
and craft exhibitions, bands,
parades, fashion shows, beach
parties and other special
events and activities all added
up to a lot of lively laughter.

But when Goombay was
phased out, Bahamians made
up for it by putting all their
pent up energy onto the already exciting Junkanoo.
Starting in the early hours of
December 26, Junkanoo is a
Bahamian-style carnival that's
guaranteed to keep you
awake. Wearing crepe paper
costumes dancers course
through the streets followed
by merrymakers carrying an
assortment of musical instru-
ments. Bugles, whistles, cow-
bells, maracas and homemade
goat-skin drums make for an
upbeat sound all of its own.
The carnival is repeated all
over again on New Year's Day.

Beat music is all the rage today for Bahamians, and tourists find the throbbing tempos infectious.

hungry slot machines, black jack, roulette, craps, baccarat and money wheels. Jackets and ties are not required, but shorts are frowned on after sundown.

Male dealers (croupiers), outfitted in tuxedos, are likely to have English accents. You may find them friendlier than you're used to in Nevada. Or you might prefer compactly costumed lady dealers.

Minimum stakes are lower on some tables in the afternoon than at night. The glittering

Levantine casino at Freeport generally has the most high-stakes ($25 or $100 minimum) blackjack tables in operation. Roulette tables have the double zero, making the odds against you even worse.

You're cautioned to take to the casino only as much money (or traveler's checks, instantly cashable) as you can afford to lose.

Casinos will be casinos: free drinks are served to seated gamblers, bars are close to the gaming area, hovering social companions are commercially available. Casino cabaret theaters feature big and brassy shows, some with dinner included.

People-to-People

To sample Bahamian life styles in a convenient, personal way, you may want to join the growing number of visitors taking advantage of this Ministry of Tourism program. Local families on New Providence or Grand Bahama entertain tourists with similar interests, perhaps at homes, churches, clubs or offices. Fill out a form obtainable from your hotel, tourist office or cruise-ship social director and you'll be put in contact with a volunteer Bahamian family. Hospitality can be overwhelming.

Dining

While the Bahamas is hardly a gourmet's paradise, local chefs do produce some interesting seafood variations, and if you're lucky you'll find a few tasty old-fashioned desserts.

Many foods are necessarily imported, frozen or otherwise, from the United States. On tourist restaurant menus, you'll find familiar American steaks and other meats. U.S. fast food chains have also invaded the Commonwealth: Nassau and Freeport sport fried chicken and hamburger outlets.

Meal prices will seem rather high to North Americans. Note that many restaurants include a 15 per cent service charge on your bill. Indifferent or somnambulant service is not unknown, but many restaurants do make an effort.

Generally restaurants serve lunch from noon to 2.30 p.m., dinner from 7 until 10 p.m. or later. Snack bars at beaches or in town are open all day.

Seafood

Conch (pronounced conk), that omnipresent chewy mollusk beloved by Bahamians, is often more admired by visitors for its decorative pink shell. But you'll want to try some or all of these proud specialities: conch chowder (creamed or with tomato), conch salad (diced conch, onions, hot red pepper, celery, sweet green pepper, cucumbers, green tomatoes), cracked conch (seasoned with lime juice, deep fried in egg and cracker crumbs), conch fritters (deep fried appetizers), conch burgers (Abaco speciality), conch cutlets, stewed conch, and other variations.

Along with standard American offerings, hotel buffets usually include a handful of native Bahamian dishes perhaps prepared with enthusiasm.

Traditionally, if not scientifically, high-protein content conch has been considered an aphrodisiac here. Conch is often eaten raw, fresh from the sea, after being extracted from the shell and cleaned. Note that the mollusk should be creamy white; never eat one which is gray with dark lips. Sad to relate, nowadays some of this staple of the Bahamian diet must be imported frozen. Every once in a while a conch pearl turns up in a shell; it may be yellow, pink or amber.

Grouper is the most popular fish in the Bahamas, served whole or in "cutlets" (it may be denied, but in some restaurants "grouper cutlets" could be shark—and just as tasty). **101**

Crawfish, most expensive seafood in the Bahamas, has two feelers instead of the claws which characterize its cousin, the northern lobster. Broiled, boiled, steamed, creamed, minced, baked, stewed, deviled or stuffed, crawfish is good eating even if it's mis-identified on many tourist menus as lobster. (Since it's illegal to catch crawfish between April 1 and July 31, you can assume it is frozen if you see it on a menu during that period.)

Crab, less expensive, is prepared in various ways, none more delicious than Andros baked crab—fresh crab meat minced, seasoned with sweet pepper and baked in its shell. You'll often see Florida stone crabs on menus, which can be delicious fresh, with mustard sauce.

Turtle steaks, stews and soups may be an acquired taste for some, but locals love them.

Shark steak and fillets from tiger shark and other shark species are rarely eaten by Bahamians although many people are surprised to find that shark is very tasty.

Other fish you find on menus include red snapper, yellowtail snapper, margarette fish (catajean) and triggerfish. They say that "boil fish," with hot red pepper, lime juice and onion, is the only true cure for a hangover. It's a big Bahamian item on Saturday and Sunday mornings. "Stew fish" with okra is another favorite.

Side Dishes

Peas 'n rice, a national passion, goes with almost anything. Imaginative chefs add grated coconut or coconut juice to the standard seasoning of onions, thyme, diced bacon, tomato paste and black pepper.

Johnny cake, another universal Bahamian favorite, is best hot from the oven, as is sweet potato bread. You might also ask for french-fried, baked or boiled sweet potatoes.

Pea soup and dumplings features a hambone or other meat, tomato and fresh hot peppers.

The best Bahamian macaroni is much spicier than the North American or Italian norm. Local grits resemble grits elsewhere.

Fruits and Desserts

If you arrive in the right season, soft and sweet Eleuthera pineapples may revolutionize your thinking about that familiar fruit. Cat Island and Long Island also grow pineapples. Try pies or tarts from the fresh fruit while you're here, and take pineapple jam or jelly home with you. Otherwise, you should sample Bahamian mangoes, sapodilla, soursop, sugar apple and, of course, coconut.

Dessert is neatly named "weight-on" around the islands. Nothing is more Bahamian than guava duff, uncompromisingly fattening but difficult to resist. This cakelike pie served with rum sauce may be the most exciting creation you'll find in island kitchens (try along Mackey Street over the hill in Nassau). "Duff sticks to your ribs," they say as you order thirds.

Grated fresh coconut goes into delicious cakes and trifles, and sometimes pudding—served warm with cream.

Carrot cake, with nuts and raisins, is another restaurant rarity, as are sapodilla ("dilly") pie and jello.

Many non-Floridian visitors will find key lime pie, with its tart flavor, an interesting new dessert.

Drinks

True to tropical traditions, rum stars on the Bahamian drinking scene. The elaborate concoctions offered by local bartenders are appealing, but sneak up on you very quickly.

Best known here, as in other hot-weather countries, is the *piña colada*, a delicious frosty blend of rum, coconut cream, pineapple juice and crushed ice. Properly, it's not shaken but mixed in a blender which gives it a milkshake-like consistency.

The top current Bahamian drink might well be a Valentine's Special from Harbour Island: pineapple rum, coconut rum and pineapple juice shaken over ice. It's very smooth and slightly frothy.

Eleuthera's pineapple rum is usually served with orange juice and ice, though fans drink it also with ginger ale, tonic, water or ice cubes.

There are about as many Goombay Smash recipes as bars, but most include regular rum, coconut rum and pineapple juice among other ingredients.

Nor do bartenders agree on a standard Bahama Mama, but you can usually count on rums, liqueur and fruit juices at least.

The Yellow Bird, probably invented at Nassau's old Royal Victoria Hotel, should have light rum, coffee and banana liqueur and fruit juices.

The Columbus Crush, a San Salvador creation, involves dark rum, Cointreau, Grand Marnier, pineapple, grapefruit, orange and lime juice. From the same island, a Skinny Minnie has rum, Cointreau, coconut liqueur, Galliano, cream

and grenadine which, after blending with crushed ice, tastes like a slightly alcoholic strawberry milkshake.

They may be gloriously iced and frosty, but too many rum drinks will not help you beat the heat.

Great Guana Cay's Guana Grabber has light, dark and coconut rum and three juices. A Paradise Smash on Paradise Island contains crème de menthe, orange liqueur, rum, crème de caçao, pineapple juice and evaporated milk. Freeport's Bahama Breeze blends dark rum, apricot brandy, banana liqueur, orange and pineapple juice.

More conventionally, you'll find ordinary rum punches (too often with tinned fruit punch), daiquiris of various flavors,

and the full range of international liquors.

The usual restaurant selection of wine (European and Californian) here is not exciting, with imported Portuguese rosés a favorite.

By world standards, American and European beers are expensive in the Bahamas because of high import duties.

Leading American soft drinks are sold everywhere. For a refreshing change, try canned sea grape soda.

BLUEPRINT for a Perfect Trip

How to Get There

Although the fares and conditions described overleaf have all been carefully checked, it is advisable to consult a travel agent for the latest information on fares and other arrangements.

From North America

BY AIR

At least a dozen American cities offer daily direct flights to Nassau, with another half dozen linked directly with Freeport. Connecting service between Nassau or Freeport is available from more than 50 cities across the United States, as well as Montreal, Edmonton, Ottawa, Regina and Winnipeg in Canada.

Charter Flights and Package Tours

Package tours for three nights or seven nights are the most popular offerings to Nassau/Paradise Island and Freeport/Lucaya or several of the Family Islands (Eleuthera, Abaco, Andros, Exuma, Walker's Cay, for example). Features of the all-inclusive packages include round-trip air transportation, transfers from and to the airport, hotel accommodations, taxes, specific tips, baggage handling and extras such as golf and tennis privileges, discount shopping books and complimentary drinks. Optional dine-around plans are available for breakfasts and dinners at different Bahamas hotels. One tour highlights a seven nights cruise through five Bahamian islands. Also popular are the combination packages featuring Miami Beach, Ft. Lauderdale or Orlando and an island in the Bahamas.

BY SEA

For those who prefer a more leisurely route, cruise-ships leave for the Bahamas from New York and from Miami or Ft. Lauderdale. There's also a rapid boat transportation between Port Everglades (Fort Lauderdale) and Freeport (travel time 2½ hours).

From the United Kingdom

BY AIR

There are several flights a week from London to Nassau and Freeport. Apart from the usual economy fares, your travel agent may be able to arrange for you to travel with a large group of individuals so that you can benefit from a special group rate. There are high and low season price differences. Reductions for children may be available. As conditions are constantly changing, check with your travel agent for the latest information.

Charter Flights and Package Tours

There are no charter flights operating to the Bahamas from the U.K., but ABC (Advance Booking Charter) and APEX fares are available to Miami, Florida, with very good onward connections to Nassau or Freeport by air and sea.

A wide variety of package holidays exist. You can cater for yourself or have full board in a comfortable hotel, and there are many variations in between these. You can even stay on two or more islands during your holiday and add excursions by air or sea to, for example, Florida or Haiti.

BY SEA

There are no regular cruise-ships or cargo/passenger boats sailing to the Bahamas from the U.K. but "fly/cruises" are quite popular. You can, for example, fly to Miami and cruise round Jamaica, Haiti and the Bahamas. There are also cruises leaving from New York (to the Bahamas and Bermuda).

From Australia

You can fly via a European gateway—London offers the widest choice of connections—or by way of the United States (see above).

From New Zealand

Choose Los Angeles or New York as your port of entry, continuing direct to Nassau from New York or via Miami from Los Angeles.

When To Go

Thanks to the Gulf Stream and trade winds, temperatures in the Bahamas are mild throughout the year. There are basically just two seasonal variations with winter (November to April) cooler and drier and summer (May to October) warmer and wetter. Despite rain and cloud now and then, a typical day has some 7 hours of sunshine. Average seawater temperatures are 75 °F (24 °C) in the winter months, 83 °F (28 °C) in the summer.

Hurricanes, which arrive (nowadays with advance warnings) on average only once every 9 years, occur between June and November.

The unprecedented snowflakes which fell one day in January, 1977 on the northern Bahamian islands have already become the stuff of legend and are regarded by experts as merely one of the many climatic aberrations affecting the world in recent years.

The following are average Nassau temperatures taken over a 20-year period.

	J	F	M	A	M	J	J	A	S	O	N	D
°F	70	70	72	75	77	80	81	82	81	78	74	7?
°C	21	21	22	24	25	27	27	28	27	26	23	2?
Rainfall (inches)	1.9	1.6	1.4	1.9	4.8	9.2	6.1	6.3	7.5	8.3	2.3	1.?

Planning Your Budget

North Americans will tend to find the Bahamas more expensive than at home. The high prices result largely from the fact that most items are imported. To give you an idea of what to expect, here is a list of average prices in Bahamian dollars based on Nassau/Paradise Island.

Airport departure tax. $10.

Barbers and hairdressers. *Man's* haircut $15, shampoo $20. *Woman's* haircut $20, wash and set $30, permanent wave $65.

Car rental (unlimited mileage). *Suzuki* $48 per day, $288 per week. *Toyota Corolla* $70 per day, $390 per week.

Cigarettes. $2.90 per pack from vending machines, less in stores.

Fishing (deep-sea charters). $300 for a boat for half day, $550 for full day.

Guided tours. City tour $12–15, tour by glass-bottomed boat $10.

Hotels (double room per person, high season, Dec.–April). *Budget range* $85. Luxury $300. Rates for single rooms only slightly lower. 7% room resort tax added to all bills.

Jitneys. In Freeport $1 in town ($4-$8 out of town), in Nassau $1.

Meals and drinks. Full hotel breakfast $10, lunch $12, dinner $20, coffee (snack bar) $2, soft drinks $2, beer $3, tropical drinks $5, spirits $5 and up.

Nightclub/Discotheques. Entry and obligatory two drinks $15, show entry $25 per person.

Sailing. Resort sunfish, small catamaran $30 per hour, parasailing $30 for 5 minutes.

Surreys. $8 per person.

Taxis (for 1 or 2 passengers). $2 for first ¼ mile and 30¢ per each additional ¼ mile.

An A–Z Summary of Practical Information and Facts

> A star (*) following an entry indicates that relevant prices are to be found on page 109.

A   **AIRPORTS*.** Nassau, Freeport and Treasure Cay (Abaco) have the only major international airports capable of handling four-engined jets and night landings. Scheduled commercial or charter flights direct from Florida land at the Family Islands of Eleuthera, San Salvador, Bimini, Exuma Cays and the Berry Islands where there are customs and immigration but only mini-airport facilities. Nassau and Freeport airports have banks, souvenir and newspaper shops, car-rental desks, tourist information counters, restaurants and snack bars.

Unless you arrive on a package tour with a pre-arranged group transfer to a hotel, you must take a taxi from either airport (there are no public buses or jitneys). Fixed taxi rates to the usual tourist destinations are posted.

On departure, U.S. customs and immigration officers at the airport give pre-clearance to passengers on flights to the U.S.

C   **CAMPING.** Camping is illegal throughout the Bahamas. One reason given is the lack of sanitary facilities on most beaches.

CAR and MOTORSCOOTER RENTAL*. See also DRIVING. In Nassau/Paradise, Grand Bahama and major Family Islands you can rent cars, with a selection ranging from standard-shift compacts to air-conditioned station wagons. American and a few European and Japanese models are available. Your home driver's license is accepted for up to three months. Without a credit card you must be 25 years old to rent a car; if you have one, 21 only. Rental cars have special white license plates so that, they quip, Bahamians will know it's a tourist driver and will be prepared for something dangerous. (Don't forget that driving here is on the left.)

A license is also required to rent a motorscooter. Crash helmets, supplied by renters, are compulsory for drivers and riders.

CHILDREN. The Bahamas is as much a paradise for children as it is for their parents. All the sights recommended in this book will be enjoyed by the kids, although some more than others, depending on their ages.

For younger children, a surrey ride round Nassau will be a change from riding round in automobiles at home, whereas older children with a little historical briefing will enjoy places like Blackbeard's Tower and other forts and monuments. The Coral World park in Nassau has a large natural underwater observatory and a series of fascinating aquariums. Youngsters dreaming of treasure can visit the Underwater Explorer's Society in Freeport which has interesting exhibits relating to divers and shipwrecks on display (see also p. 38). Also in Freeport, while shoppers choose gifts in the International Bazaar for friends back home, the kids can find ice-cream. pizzas, hamburgers, hot dogs and sodas to keep them happy.

Most major hotels have some arrangements for children, particularly in the summer. These include organized beach games, afternoon movies, bingo, etc. Some hotels have babysitter service; check with the social hostess.

CIGARETTES, CIGARS, TOBACCO*. In Nassau and Freeport you'll find the entire range of American tobacco products. There are also Cuban and some European cigars, as well as a few European brands of cigarettes and pipe tobacco on sale. The selection is more limited on the Family Islands.

CLOTHING. Lightweight, casual clothing is all most tourists will need in the Bahamas. For dining at better restaurants, men might want to pack a sports jacket and tie, women a cocktail dress or smart pants suit. Sandals, shorts, sunglasses, rugged shoes for hiking, and sunshades or caps are useful. Rainwear is not usually necessary.

COMMUNICATIONS

Post offices, often very modest affairs on Family Islands, operate for some or all of normal working hours Monday through Friday and on Saturday morning. Hotel gift shops may also sell stamps. Mail incoming to the Bahamas is normally sent to post office boxes—your hotel will have one. Postal service is erratic: mail to or from the United States might take as little as three days, as long as two weeks. Mail to or from Europe could take even longer, or be amazingly speedy.

Telegrams and telex: Nassau and Freeport have direct telex communications with most of the world, meaning quick service in major hotels with their own telex machines. A three-minute minimum is charged **111**

C for telexes. Telegrams are sent via international commercial companies, telephoned through Nassau or Freeport from the Family Islands. Letter telegrams (LT) with a minimum of 22 words, which arrive the following morning, are much cheaper.

Telephone: The Bahamas, with Caribbean area code 809, is included in the North American telephone network. From the major resort islands, there is direct distance dialing (DDD) to North America, Hawaii, Jamaica, Puerto Rico, Virgin Islands, Bermuda and major Mexican cities. Certain Family Islands can receive but not initiate DDD calls. From hotels in Nassau/Paradise and Freeport, tourists must go through the Batelco (Bahamas Telecommunications Corporation) operator, but calls to North America or Europe usually take just a few minutes. From some Family Islands there is direct dialing to Nassau but often local operators are on duty only for a certain number of daylight hours. Radio telephone service to yachts is available from Nassau and major marinas.

COMPLAINTS. For on-the-spot problem solving, the manager of the hotel, marina, restaurant or shop should be able to help. Otherwise, the Visitor Relations Unit (see below), takes care of both written and telephoned complaints. Tourist information offices in Nassau and Freeport may also be helpful. In some cases, you might refer either to the Chamber of Commerce or the Bahamas Hotel Association. For serious problems, contact the police.

Visitor Relations Unit, Ministry of Tourism, P.O. Box N-3701, Nassau; tel. 322-7500.

COURTESIES. Bahamians are much too relaxed to insist on formal social niceties, but as in most small communities they expect people to say hello or acknowledge them even in passing—friendly behavior which may seem odd to big city visitors. Driving around the Family Islands especially, you'll notice people waving to you and to everybody else. Tourists should not interpret the reserve or shyness of many Bahamians as deliberate rudeness or hostility. Once engaged in friendly conversation, most islanders will prove courteous and helpful.

If you're invited to a Bahamian home, it's not customary to take your own bottle (parties usually feature an abundance of food and drink), though flowers or a small gift for the hostess would not be out of place.

Do not wear bathing suits at indoor restaurants or in downtown **112** Nassau and Freeport.

CRIME. In Nassau/Paradise, crime has become a matter of concern to police and tourism authorities. While the amount of petty theft, break-in robbery and other crimes might seem rather small to urban Americans, many Europeans may be shocked. Efforts to stem crime (some of it drug-related and some affecting tourists) are being made in this most-crowded center of the Bahamas. Common sense precautions include: locking valuables in your hotel's safe deposit boxes; not leaving anything important in your rented car even if locked, and not walking after dark in dubious areas except perhaps in a group. Bimini, though tiny, also has a considerable crime problem. The situation is quite different in Freeport (where crime is much less frequent), and incomparable in the other Family Islands where honesty is so taken for granted that many people still don't bother to lock their doors.

C

DIVING IN THE BAHAMAS. There are hundreds of places to dive throughout the archipelago. The list below gives a summary of some of the best sites off the islands discussed in this book.

D

Abaco. Reef off Walker's Cay (diving only about seven months a year); underwater caves; Fowl Cay and Pelican Cay underwater parks; the Civil War wreck *U. S. S. Adirondack* near Marsh Harbour; exceptional reef off Hole in the Wall in the south.

Andros. Magnificent drop-off and crevice diving with large fish along a 20-mile Andros reef, where groupers, red hinds and moray eels watch a sunken World War II landing barge 70 feet down off Small Hope Bay; lush and coral at shallow Love Hill Channel; best coral sights are probably at Green Cay south of Fresh Creek; Sea Turtle Ridge; outstanding photography at Valley of the Sponges; inside the great reef are many blue holes and elkhorn coral stands; most thrilling shallow viewing of fish and spongers is off mouth of Lisbon Creek in South Bight; Linda Cay Blue Hole, "Big Grunter Hole," "Grunt Show" and "Boiling Hole"; many fish and good coral formations at "Hen and Chicken" reef off Nicoll's Town in the north; sharks, dolphins, etc., along the long ledge of the Tongue of the Ocean.

Berry Islands. Marvelous shallowish reef off Mamma Rhoda Rock close to Chub Cay marinas with thousands of small fish; drop-off diving with black coral and large rays.

Bimini. Top diving with minimum 90 feet visibility at Victories Reef, stretching 5 miles off South Cat Cay; spectacular drift diving along Bimini wall of the continental shelf, also various sunken wrecks, partly exposed; curious rock formations inspiring the "Atlantis" theory are only 15 feet down; Turtle Rock off South Bimini for grunts and turtles.

D **Cat Island.** Fine wall diving off southern coast, large schools of fish an many crawfish in shallower reefs; nearly virgin coral formations o island's northwestern coast.

Eleuthera. In north, wrecks, coral, fish and turtles around Devil Backbone reef off Spanish Wells and Harbour Island; off Glass Win dow, the "Plateau" with all types of coral; fast drift dive throug Current Cut, with schools of large barracudas, groupers, eagle rays an jacks; shallow reefs and resort diving sites off Winding Bay; the famou Eleuthera wall off Cape Eleuthera is a beautiful, steep drop-off div with unusual sponges and coral.

Exumas. Varied marine life in Stocking Island's ocean blue hole oppo site George Town and other undersea caves in the area; at Staniel Ca is the huge "Thunderball Grotto" (from the James Bond movie through the Exuma Cays Land and Sea Park up to Highbourn Cay outstanding shallow reefs with the entire coral family, sponges an great swarms of fish; a mile-long vertical bank of coral at Wax Cay Cu south of now-private Norman's Cay, among the finest shallow dives i the Bahamas.

Grand Bahama. Good deep diving along the reef for 60 miles east o Bell Channel, many types of coral; excellent snorkeling on shallov reefs; open-water blue holes teem with fish; inland Ben's Cave is a blu hole with stalactites; site of Lucayan treasure find; spectacular grottoe friendly fish near an 80-foot reef southwest of Indian Cay light at th West End; shallower reefs in this area are excellent for photography.

Long Island. Dramatic photography at Shark Reef off Stella Mari when sharks are attracted for feeding; fish, coral and caves at Groupe Village; schools of large blue tangs and many other species cruise th four-acre Blue Tang Reef; in calm weather, splendid elkhorn and othe varieties at Coral Gardens; overhangs, coral stands, caves and (some times) friendly barracuda at Barracuda Heads; accessible from Stell Maris: Dave's Wall at Conception Island, for dives to huge caves an channels, with black coral and sponges, and Southampton Reef (Con ception Island) with a large World War II wreck amid beautiful elkhor coral. Rum Cay Wall features tremendous fish variety and 19th-centur wreck of *H. M. S. Ocean Conqueror*, the first British screw-driven battle ship.

New Providence. Best shallow or deep diving is along the drop-off a Goulding Cay off the western tip of New Providence. Here, novic scuba divers and snorkelers are taken to reefs along Rose Island with certain amount of interesting marine life; other tours go to th *Mahoney* wreck near Nassau harbor and to an ocean hole 7 miles ou

San Salvador. An increasingly "in" location for the international diving crowd; "La Crevasse" at French Bay in the southwest may be the finest single dive in the Bahamas, a deep canyon with magnificent coral, huge fish and a drop-off from 60 to 6,000 feet; some two dozen other dive sites in the reef area from Sandy Point up to Cockburn Town, including shallow "Snapshot Reef" where snorkelers, too, enjoy the high coral heads and resident goat fish; other good reefs off the southeastern corner of the island; underwater visibility around San Salvador is usually between 150 and 200 feet.

Note: If you'd like to search for the hundreds of millions of dollars worth of treasure believed sunk in the Bahamas, some professionals say the best bet should be along the western edge of the Great Bahama bank all the way from Great Isaac Light to the Old Bahama Channel near Cuba.

DRIVING IN THE BAHAMAS. Probably the Commonwealth's most noticeable reminder of the British era is driving on the left. But most cars in the Bahamas, products of or targeted for the American market, have the steering wheel on the left side. This makes it difficult to see around slow-moving trucks in order to pass ("Undertakers love Overtakers" reads a sign in Freeport). At roundabouts (traffic circles), drive around to the left but yield to traffic coming around from the right.

Roads in the Bahamas range from reasonable to poor. The speed limit in built-up areas is 25 miles per hour, and generally 30 m.p.h. elsewhere except for a few divided highway stretches in Nassau and Freeport where 45 m.p.h. is posted. The two major centers have traffic lights and some formal crosswalks.

You're likely to see dangerous, even wild driving in the Bahamas, probably most often by young people. The many large American cars are not well suited to the generally narrow Bahamian roads which they share with motorscooters, bicycles, limousine taxis, trucks, jitneys and, in Nassau, horse surreys. Children and animals are also a hazard and often dart onto the roads. Rush hour traffic on New Providence and over the Paradise Island bridge is well worth avoiding. In the few areas where parking is a problem, you'll find spaces or lots clearly identified.

Breakdowns and Fuel: Service stations with mechanics are adequate on New Providence and Grand Bahama, harder to find elsewhere. If you have a breakdown, your rental car agency should provide an emergency telephone number through which either a mechanic or a substitute car can be arranged. Gas is not normally a problem.

D **DRUGS.** Lying conveniently between Colombia and the United States, the Bahamian islands with their deserted coves and unpatrolled airstrips are transit points for an enormous amount of illegal marijuana and cocaine. Some of these drugs are used clandestinely in the Bahamas, and pushers on occasion accost tourists in such spots as Nassau, Paradise Island, Bimini and Freeport. But there are severe penalties ranging up to 10 years in jail and a $5,000 fine for peddling or using any dangerous drug including marijuana. Bahamian narcotics officials are particularly vigilant against the importing of drugs by tourists.

E **ELECTRIC CURRENT.** The Bahamas has standard North American current, 120 volts, 60 cycles A.C.

EMBASSIES and CONSULATES. Only a few countries maintain formal diplomatic posts in Nassau:

Britain: British High Commission, BITCO Building, 3rd Floor, East Street, P.O. Box N-7516, Nassau; tel. 325-7471 (after hours 326-6222).

United States: Embassy, Queen Street, Mosmar Building, P.O. Box N-8197, Nassau; tel. 322-1181.

ENTRY FORMALITIES and CUSTOMS CONTROLS. All visitors must fill in a brief immigration card on arrival, keeping the carbon copy to surrender when leaving the country. Americans may enter the Bahamas as bona fide visitors for up to eight months, Britons and Canadians for three weeks, if they have evidence of citizenship (birth certificate or voter's card), a return or onward ticket from the Bahamas and enough funds to cover their stay. U.K. and Canadian citizens need passports to stay longer than three weeks. U.S. citizens returning home are pre-cleared by U.S. customs and immigration officers at Nassau and Freeport international airports.

West European and South American citizens with passports may enter the Bahamas as visitors for varying lengths of time without visas, providing they have prepaid onward or return transportation. Currently no health certificates are required for entry into the Bahamas. There is a departure tax for everyone over the age of three leaving the country (see p. 108).

Your baggage declaration on entry into the Bahamas is verbal unless you have dutiable items, in which case you complete a form. The procedure is usually swift.

The following chart shows what main duty-free items you may take into the Bahamas and, when returning home, into your own country:

Into:	Cigarettes		Cigars		Tobacco	Spirits		Wine
Bahamas	200	or	50	or	1 lb.	1 qt.	and	1 qt.
Australia	200	or	250 g.	or	250 g.	1 l.	or	1 l.
Canada	200	and	50	and	900 g.	1.1 l.	or	1.1 l.
Eire	200	or	50	or	250 g.	1 l.	and	2 l.
N. Zealand	200	or	50	or	½ lb.	1 qt.	and	1 qt.
S. Africa	400	and	50	and	250 g.	1 l.	and	1 l.
U.K.	200	or	100	or	500 g.	1 l.	and	2 l.
U.S.A.	200	and	100	and	*	1 l.	or	1 l.

* a reasonable quantity

Currency restrictions: Foreign currency may be imported or exported in unlimited amounts. You may also bring into and take out of the islands local currency up to a maximum of Bahamian $70 per person.

GUIDES and INTERPRETERS. Guides employed by commercial tour agencies and some qualified taxi drivers take groups of various sizes around New Providence/Paradise Island and Grand Bahama. Certain hotels have their own tour guides. There are a small number of interpreters in Nassau and Freeport who can speak primarily Spanish, German and French (check with the Ministry of Tourism), and a very few Out Island hotels with staff able to speak such foreign languages.

HEALTH and HAZARDS, These are generally healthy islands, with about 50 scattered clinics and three major hospitals—Princess Margaret and Rassin (known as the Doctor's Hospital) in Nassau and Rand Memorial in Freeport—trying to keep them that way. Your hotel should have a doctor or nurse on call. In addition, medical evacuation flights, some direct to Florida, can be arranged from all resort islands. Many settlements have pharmacies.

H   Too much sun and too much rum are far and away the major cause of tourist distress in the Bahamas. The obvious answer is to avoid over-exposure ashore or even in the sea, and to forego over-indulgence in bartender exotica.

Mosquitoes can be bothersome in hot weather, but worse are the infamous sand-flies (known variously as midges, "no-see-ums", "flying teeth", etc.). When they're out in force, these tiny terrors ignore screens, air-conditioning and creams.

On land, neither the many snakes of the Bahamas nor any other reptiles or animals are poisonous. On the other hand, centipedes which grow to six inches or longer, like to come indoors and their sting can cause illness. Ground spiders, a form of tarantula, look gruesome but they're slow-moving, easily spotted and don't pack much venom in their bite. Highly toxic black widows keep to themselves in generally inaccessible places.

In the sea, the spines of barbed sea urchins are painful and difficult to remove. The best remedy is to use hot candle wax or other heat to draw them out and soothe pain; locals say urine is also a good cure. As outlined in the Scuba Diving section (p. 87), divers will want to avoid certain corals and other immobile menaces, as well as sharks, sting rays, moray eels and a few other unfriendly creatures.

If you're catching your own dinner, be sure you know or can consult a Bahamian expert about which fish not to eat. Several species are definitely toxic, causing the serious illness of ciguatera which has long plagued tropical waters.

Don't eat "Samba conch"—old conch with mossy shells, or with gray instead of creamy white flesh.

To cover your expenses in case of accident or illness while on holiday, you should take out special insurance before leaving home.

HITCHHIKING. Hitchhiking is not advisable in the Bahamas and, in any case, is illegal.

HOTELS and ACCOMMODATIONS*. Accommodations in these islands range from wooden-slatted, breeze-cooled little guest houses through double-deck houseboats with saunas on to elegantly appointed hotel suites with silent air-conditioning. In the recent tourist boom many hotels have been full throughout the high season, from mid-December to April, despite prices significantly higher than during the rest of the year. But with the exception of a few very popular resorts

Family Island places are less jammed throughout the year than Nassau/Paradise and Grand Bahama.

Hotel packages may include no meals (EP—European Plan), breakfast and dinner (MAP—Modified American Plan), or all meals (AP—American Plan). Only rarely will you encounter the European bed-and-breakfast concept. If you're vacationing at a remote Family Island hotel, it's usually wise to opt at least for MAP. But in Nassau, Paradise Island and Freeport you'll have a choice of many restaurants outside your hotel. Some Bahamian hotels offer watersports, golf and tennis packages which you book from abroad.

For those who like to do their own cooking, New Providence/Paradise and Freeport/Lucaya have a variety of cottages, villas and condominium units for vacation rental, often with maid service. These, too, should be booked well in advance for the winter months.

LANGUAGE. The Bahamian dialect is a constant source of amusement and confusion for visitors. Listening in around the islands, you'll hear a fascinating verbal concert, featuring traces of Caribbean and West African creole, U.S. English and old time pirate speech, not to mention British colonial phrases and current American disco slang. Different islands have their own linguistic peculiarities. You'll doubtless have to ask for a translation now and then, which Bahamians will cheerfully try to provide.

Nothing is more common than *axe*, as in "What he axe you?" (What did he ask you?). *V* is very often pronounced as *w*, as in "They is divorced". The meaning of some phrases is more or less clear: "She have scattery teeth"; "Hungry killing me"; "I be born here".

Very common in this churchgoing country is the phrase, "If God spare life", used to reply to such things as "See you tomorrow".

Ask a Family Islander where the local action is and you might hear, "Dance and church always be full".

For right away or soon, Bahamians use "terreckly"—but don't count on it.

"You shake man hand, you no shake him heart" means you can't tell what someone is like if you meet him only casually.

If you wonder why someone slept late, try "Why you sleep on your rent smorning?" And to console somebody going through a bad period: "Every rope have an end."

LAUNDRY and DRY-CLEANING. Although there are "laundry mats" and cleaners in larger Bahamian settlements, most tourists will

L find it more convenient to handle this through their hotel, perhaps making a private agreement with a maid. Major marinas have washing machines for yacht people.

LOST and FOUND. Try the police. Taxi drivers and other Bahamians do turn in things they find.

M **MAPS.** The Lands and Surveys office on Bay Street, Nassau, produces and sells inexpensively the best maps and charts of the Commonwealth, aside from the detailed marine charts found in such specialist publications as the annual *Yachtsman's Guide to the Bahamas*. Free commercial or Ministry of Tourism maps, mostly of New Providence and Paradise Island, are more or less adequate for visitors needs. A few hotels have produced good maps of their own Family Islands.

MEETING PEOPLE. Particularly in the Family Islands which have experienced less tourism, Bahamians tend to be initially shy with strangers. But once you make the first friendly approach, you're usually swamped with cheerful chatter and hospitality. Smiling is much in fashion around these islands. Young and not so young people engage in a good deal of easygoing flirting, and there's no reason why tourists shouldn't join in. You'll meet Bahamians easily almost everywhere (not at casinos where they're forbidden to gamble), but to be put in contact with people who share your special interests, you might try the much-praised People-to-People program (see p. 99).

MONEY MATTERS

Currency: The Bahamian dollar is pegged to U.S. currency (which is used interchangeably around the Commonwealth), and divided into 100 cents. These coins circulate: 1, 5, 10, 15, 25 and 50 cents and $1, $2, $3 and $5. Bills: 50¢, $1, $3, $5, $10, $20, $50 and $100. Souvenir hunters are reducing the number of fluted dimes, square 15¢ pieces, $2 coins and $3 bills. Because of conversion difficulty abroad, it's wise to convert any Bahamian money into U.S. dollars before you leave the country. For currency restrictions, see ENTRY FORMALITIES AND CUSTOMS CONTROLS.

Banking hours (Nassau and Freeport): 9:30 a.m. to 3 p.m. Monday through Thursday, to 5 p.m. on Fridays, closed weekends and holidays.

Changing money: While there are some foreign exchange facilities, European, South American and other non-North American visitors will save trouble by arriving with U.S. dollars and dollar traveler's checks rather than other currency. Canadian dollars are exchangeable in the Bahamas, but the rate may not be very advantageous.

Traveler's Checks and Credit Cards: Major international traveler's checks are easily cashed at Bahamian hotels, shops, restaurants and casinos. Personal checks are not generally accepted, but credit cards are usually honored.

NEWSPAPERS and MAGAZINES. Nassau's two daily newspapers (the morning *Guardian* and the afternoon *Tribune*) appear Monday through Saturday and sometimes turn up a day or two later in the Family Islands. The modest *Freeport News* comes out Monday through Friday. Abaco's Chamber of Commerce has begun the *Abaco Life*, an interesting if infrequent newspaper for tourists about that large Family Island cluster. In Nassau and Freeport, the *New York Times, Wall Street Journal* and *Miami Herald* are usually available on the day of publication; European and Canadian periodicals are scarcer. American news weeklies and many feature magazines are widely sold.

PETS. To import your animal, you'll need a Bahamian government permit, general health and rabies certificates and money to pay a special duty charge. Pets may only be brought in by air, to Freeport or Nassau, and must immediately be revaccinated. For a short vacation, it hardly seems worth it—and not all hotels would accept a pet.

PHOTOGRAPHY. Buy your film at home—it's expensive in the Bahamas. Nassau has film processing outlets which will do prints in one hour. Four slides and black-and-white, you'll want to wait until you get home. Keep your camera and film in cool, shady places as much as possible. Because of the strong sun and glare from sea and sand, filters are almost essential for decent photography. Beach shots are often best in the late afternoon. Sunsets make spectacular pictures.

POLICE. Underworked on most Family Islands but busy in Nassau, the friendly and helpful Bahamian police sport black trousers or skirts with red stripes and white short-sleeved shirts.
Emergency police numbers: 919 and 24444 (in Nassau).

P PUBLIC HOLIDAYS

January 1	New Year's Day
Friday before Easter	Good Friday
Monday after Easter	Easter Monday
First Friday in June	Labor Day
Seventh Monday after Easter	Whit Monday
July 10	Independence Day
First Monday in August	Emancipation Day
October 12 (if weekend, nearest Friday or Monday)	Discovery Day
December 25	Christmas Day
December 26	Boxing Day

R RADIO and TV.
ZNS, the Bahamas national broadcasting system, has three radio services: a "network" for the entire country, an AM-FM station for New Providence, and a separate Grand Bahama transmission. ZNS television, channel 13, is beamed from Nassau and seen on Grand Bahama, Andros and Eleuthera. Parts of the Commonwealth pick up Florida TV stations with varying reception. Satellite TV is offered at many of the major hotels. This enables you to see programs from a variety of channels from the U.S. mainland. South Florida radio stations are heard loud and clear in the Bahamas.

On short wave, American, Canadian, BBC, German, French, Spanish and Russian broadcasts can be heard in the Bahamas, reception best between dusk and dawn.

RELIGIOUS SERVICES. Religion is alive, well and everywhere in the Bahamas. Denominations include: Anglican, Baptist, Christian Science, Church of God, Hebrew Congregation, Jehovah's Witnesses, Lutheran, Methodist, Plymouth Brethren, Presbyterian, Roman Catholic and Seventh Day Adventist.

T TIME DIFFERENCES.
U.S. Eastern Standard Time prevails on all the Bahama islands, and Eastern Daylight Saving Time is adopted in the summer when the Americans do.

Los Angeles	Chicago	New York	**Bahamas**	London
9 a.m.	11 a.m.	noon	**noon**	5 p.m.

TIPPING. At many hotels and restaurants a service charge is automatically added to the bill to cover gratuities. Ask if you are unsure. Some tipping recommendations:

Barber/Hairdresser	15%
Lavatory attendant	50¢–$1
Porter, per bag	$1
Taxi/Surrey driver	15–20%
Tourist guide	15–20% of tour cost
Waiter	15% if service charge not included

TOILETS. Facilities marked Men or Women, occasionally indicated by symbols, are found in restaurants, hotels, bars, certain stores and public buildings, at marinas and airfields.

TOURIST INFORMATION OFFICES. In Nassau there are tourist information offices at the airport, at Rawson Square and at Prince George Wharf (tel. 69781 or 69772) downtown. In Freeport/Lucaya: at the International Bazaar and the airport (tel. 352-8044). Bahamas Tourist Offices abroad:

Canada:

Montreal	1255 Philips Square, Montreal, Que. H3B3G1; tel. (514) 861-6797.
Toronto	85 Richmond Street West, Toronto, Ont. M5H2C9; tel. (416) 363-4441.
Vancouver	470 Grandville Street, Vancouver, B.C. V6C1V5; tel. (604) 688-8334.

United Kingdom:

London	10, Chesterfield Street, London WIX 8AH; tel. (071) 629-5238.

United States:

Atlanta	1950 Century Boulevard NE, Suite 26, Atlanta, GA 30345; tel. (404) 633-1793.
Boston	1027 Statler Office Building, Boston, MA 02116; tel. (617) 426-3144.

Chicago	875 North Michigan Avenue, Chiago, IL. 60611; tel. (312) 787-8203.
Dallas	World Trade Center, Suite 186, P.O. Box 581408, Dallas, TX 75201; tel. (214) 742-1886.
Detroit	26400 Lahser Road, Suite 112 A, Southfield, MI 48034; tel. (313) 357-2940.
Houston	5177 Richmond Avenue, Suite 755, Houston, TX 77056; tel. (713) 626-1566.
Los Angeles	3450 Wilshire Boulevard, Los Angeles, CA 90010; tel. (213) 385-0033.
Miami	255 Alhambra Circle, Coral Gables, FL 33134; tel. (305) 442-4860.
New York	150 East 52 Street, New York, NY 10022; tel. 757-1611.
Philadelphia	LaFayette Building, 437 Chestnut Street, Room 216, Philadelphia, PA 19106; tel. (212) 925-0871.
San Francisco	44 Montgomery Street, Suite 503, San Francisco, CA 94104; tel. (415) 398-5502.
St. Louis	555, North Ballas, Suite 310, St. Louis, MO 63141; tel. (314) 569-7777.
Washington DC	1730 Rhode Island Avenue, NW Washington DC 20036; tel. (202) 659-9135.

TRANSPORTATION

Taxis*: Partly because distances are considerable between places on New Providence/Paradise and on other islands, taxi fares seem high to many visitors. Taxi drivers have a near-monopoly of transportation at airports and some remote hotels. You should normally insist that the meter be started, although fares from important airports to usual destinations are posted. Sightseeing taxi tours may be negotiated. There are now more than 500 taxis in New Providence/Paradise, far fewer on other islands. Beware of "hackers", private vehicle owners who cruise illegally for passengers and charge more than taxis. Their cars are not marked "taxi". Some cab drivers have passed a "know your country" course run by the Ministry of Tourism, displaying a "Bahamahost" decal or badge which indicates their ability to help tourists.

Jitneys*: In the absence of public buses, the budget way to get around New Providence (where walking isn't feasible), is by minibus, called jitney locally, for which you wait at designated bus stops. This is basic native transportation not geared for tourists, but it's a good way to mingle with Bahamians and to see residential areas. Frederick Street off downtown Day Street is a major jitney depot. Jitneys don't go to Paradise Island (hotels there provide transportation to downtown Nassau and there are also ferries across the channel).

Surreys: At or near Rawson Square in Nassau you can hire a horse surrey for a set hourly rate (bargaining doesn't work). Except during rush hour when traffic and fumes prevail, this is a pleasantly relaxed way to tour the downtown area, with your surrey driver pointing out highlights in his best Bahamian. In the summer months, regulations now forbid owners to operate surreys between 1 and 4 p.m.—the hottest time of the day.

Mail boats: If you have the time, stamina and sense of adventure, mail boats are the cheapest way to reach the Family Islands. Almost all of these cargo-carrying boats leave weekly from either Potters Cay or Prince George Wharf in Nassau, and voyage to all the major islands as well as many of the cays. The length of the journey depends not only on distance but also weather conditions, with most trips lasting between four and 14 hours. An up-to-date list of mail-boat services will be available from the Ministry of Tourism in Nassau, but it's essential to check departure time and space availability personally with the captain (although ZNS radio broadcasts expected daily schedules). Then get to the dock well in advance to be sure you have a reasonable place to sit (passengers find themselves perching on live turtles, bundles of frozen fish and other unlikely items jammed onto mail boats). Many families regularly send "the box" by mail boat to relatives on other islands, which can mean anything from a cardboard carton to a huge gunnysack.

Chartered planes: Small planes can be chartered at various airfields including Nassau and Freeport for inter-island transportation. If your Family Island doesn't have a plane on hand, call one of the charter companies in Nassau and they'll send one out.

WATER. It's generally safe to drink tap water in the Bahamas, but most visitors won't particularly like the taste. Much local water comes from wells in limestone rock, accounting for a distinct "limey" flavor. Purified drinking water in bottles or plastic containers is sold widely. There's a serious water shortage on many Family Islands and cays and even, at times, on New Providence (which barges in fresh water from Andros).

Index

An asterisk (*) next to a page number indicates a map reference.